Are You a Civil Servant

While every precaution has been taken in the preparation of this book, the publisher assumes no responsibility for errors or omissions, or for damages resulting from the use of the information contained herein.

ARE YOU A CIVIL SERVANT

First edition. March 29, 2024.

Copyright © 2024 Yeong Hwan Choi.

ISBN: 979-8224207701

Written by Yeong Hwan Choi.

Table of Contents

https://brunch.co.kr/@edaf6c3031c5401

Are You a Civil Servant

Yeong Hwan Choi

For the readers of the book

Is the resignation of MZ civil servants in South Korea a social trend? Or is it a problem that will be gradually resolved as the environment changes, such as improving organizational culture, increasing salaries, and the way society views civil servants? Based on the story of two years at a large company and seven years in a civil service organization, I analyzed why the resignation rate of young civil servants is so high according to human instinct and brain science. I believe that there is not much difference between not only ordinary civil servants, but also public companies and teachers and police officers who are guaranteed tenure, and I decided to write a book to inform the students who are preparing for the civil service examination just because they want to enjoy a stable life without having time to get to know themselves, and to inform those who are preparing to change jobs in the civil service after leaving a large company to make a judgment without experiencing it.

The change in organizational culture is a phenomenon that naturally changes when the younger generation joins, and even if a lot of improvement ideas are introduced, it is not a problem in terms of the supply and demand of civil service jobs. Therefore, the government will not be interested in the future. It is said that there are people in the world who know without experiencing it, people who have experienced it and know it, and people who have experienced it but do not know. As someone who has experienced and enlightened me, I can only hope that the examinees will not follow the same path as me.

Are you a civil servant?

In 2015, my lazy brain challenged me to take the civil service exam, which I thought would be advantageous for marriage and a stable life with a small salary, as my lazy brain was guaranteed to work, and I moved to a civil service job in a large company in the eyes of others. Even before I joined a large company, I had chosen a job that others thought was good in a subject that was my major in college. I don't know what I like, what I'm good at, or what I don't like. Of course, I haven't experienced it, so even if I didn't know, I think I didn't ask specific questions about myself.

And it wasn't until I was thirty-five after I left the company that I was filling in my own self one by one on a blank sheet of white paper. Valued existence in your own way, not from other people's perspectives and perspectives. If we go back in time, after leaving a large company, I was satisfied with my life as a civil servant. My work-life balance is much better than it used to be. There was little competition for performance, and I was satisfied that I could only take care of my own personal affairs and that it was easier for me to live a life of self-improvement or evening. But my lazy brain didn't want to progress. I could have worked as a civil servant if I had a different perspective on success, but I intuitively knew I had to get out of here. But this phenomenon has started to become a social issue, and are they people who have the same values as me? Or why did they make the same choice as me?

Chapter 1: If You Dislike the Temple, Leave the Monks

The world is in the age of the weak and strong.

Humans are also animals, and their intelligence is relatively high, but their instincts are similar. Just as powerful nations have historically and even now wielded world politics at will, so too is the small society in which we live. Individuals who are weaker than the organization are forced to conform or leave. Now, it is common to hear that it is a one-person business and that the concept of a lifelong job has disappeared. We are living in a very good era where you can show your personality and color with a platform released with just a computer or mobile phone, and you can start a business with a single computer.

However, as a child, I lost my own color even more without forming an identity that should have been formed due to numerous worries and experiences. The motivation for my resignation can be seen as the need for self-actualization, which is at a higher level of human needs.

When I started questioning my self-existence by starting with philosophical doubts such as 'Who am I?' and 'What am I working for here?', I gradually felt that something was wrong in my fifth year as a civil servant. The growing pains are gone. Before going to bed and even when I woke up, I wished I had been hit by a car and killed when it was time to go to work, and I just waited for the time at work to get off work. I didn't feel alive in this dark place. I wanted to break free from the cycle of evil.

Live zombies.

Not only civil servants, but also large corporations, public corporations, and foreign companies favored by job seekers, if they do not change their mindset and perspective on success, most of them will live their lives as passive workers as they accumulate years of service.

And these wage slaves become living zombies over time. As a helpless being who has no choice but to live within the framework set by society....

Homeless people on the streets are no exception. Money and food are important to them, but the feeling of being alone and abandoned in the world is what bothers them the most. If you help them feel their presence in the world with an altruistic heart rather than financial help, Steve Jobs and Elon Musk can come out of it. Everyone has potential in the realm of the unconscious, and whether or not they realize their potential depends on how they live their lives away from work. It's only after 10 years of salary slavery that I've started reading, writing, and starting the business I want to do, that I'm slowly realizing it. People should take the time to get to know themselves with a high sense of purpose in life. And through the time you have learned, you can only become less faint by choosing a job that resembles your own color, which is a tendency that has been established according to your innate temperament and environment (family, friends, education, etc.).

So I decided to leave in my eighth year to find color.

1.1 Their Exclusive League

At the age of 28, my first assignment was to the Construction Management Headquarters in the city hall, which is dominated by civil engineers. This department is responsible for ordering projects and executing budgets for the purpose of opening and expanding roads, which are convenient facilities for citizens. There are many miscellaneous things such as continuous design changes and actual accidents, but to explain it simply, he was in charge of supervising the construction company and managing the budget so that it could be used efficiently. Rather than dealing with the actual civil engineering technology, my work was mainly focused on writing reports, including a technical review in which the contractor analyzed how the budget would change. My two-year experience at a construction company was very helpful when I went to the site to supervise, but my classmates, who were new civil servants, felt a little disconnect between what they had learned at university and what they had learned. As I will say later, civil service jobs are not highly professional. Aside from technical jobs, my classmates were of course administrative officials, and I worked in the office a lot from the beginning.

When we became civil servants, there was a severe civil service boom in society. My younger siblings, who were born after the mid-90s, preferred large corporations and public companies, but we had a lot of people who were less prepared to become civil servants because of the social atmosphere that favored state institutions more. Although I didn't study at Noryangjin after leaving a large company, Noryangjin cupbap and gongdangi were common words in news and articles. It was so popular, and because of that, **it was a bizarre era when even among the ninth class, SKY accounted for 5% of those who passed.** There were a lot of people in the 9th grade administrative positions who had more than an academic background in Chongqing, so how hard it was for liberal arts students to get a job, so why would they look at the 9th grade? I thought about that a lot at the time.

Of course, people with good education would quickly quit and go to take the professional exams, but the reason why I want to tell you that people with good education studied the ninth grade was that it was quite popular at the time, and **no one wanted to become a civil servant without any specific reason for why they wanted to become a civil servant, so I think the "goodbye everyone" resignation boom over the years ended up as well.** After becoming a civil servant, the difference between them and private companies is that they are more and more in a league of their own. Of course, there are only two main ways that office workers can be compensated. Promotion and remuneration.

However, civil servants are increasingly unable to find their value in anything other than promotion. From the outside, whether he is in the ninth grade, the seventh grade, or the fifth level, he is just a civil servant. Unfortunately, they apply their highest priority to the reward system of promotion.

Here's why they're looking for a promotion:

1. A salary the size of a rat's tail goes up by a rat's tail.

2. You can do things with words rather than with your own actions.

3. Even though you're your boss, you don't take on responsibilities as much as you think.

In addition to this, civil servants did little self-development. There were quite a few people who didn't see their careers differently from their previous colleagues who had built their careers through various challenges and experiences, but they were still in their jobs and getting paid overtime. The practice of subsistence overtime has disappeared a lot since when I joined the company, but it is difficult to change the culture all at once, and it is understandable if you are a father with children. However, some of the young civil servants who were aware of the damage were forced to work overtime, and it was a waste of time to work in the evening. Unlike those who were trying to find their colors after work, they even looked pathetic.

Of course, there are many cases where government employees work on an emergency basis because they have tasks that require weather conditions (rain, snow) or emergencies (forest fires). And each serial has a different degree of difficulty and intensity of work. The work of technical and administrative officials, except for civil engineering and architectural officials, is often simple and repetitive administration and civil complaint handling, so it can be considered that the degree of difficulty is low unless it is a planning department. After passing, the brain capacity used is not half the brain used for the college major assignments you studied, the brain needed to pass the exam, or the brain you worked for a company. Even though they know that each other is a group that lacks expertise, no one is engaged in self-improvement. The reason for this is that there are many things that you naturally know over time, so if you ask them to get to know you through working overtime, the difficulty of the work is so low that you think it is only a way to make a living, or to look good to your bosses.

If you are a civil engineer, if you go to a department related to urban development or urban planning, you will have to deal with the legal interpretation given by the Ministry of Legislation, which can sometimes be a headache. In situations where the law, enforcement ordinance, enforcement regulations, and city ordinances are unclear or in conflict with each other, they should consult a lawyer, or if the situation is not a relatively large budget or is far from the commitment of the head of the agency, the matter should be handled as a matter of practice.

This is also a legal interpretation for administrative processing, so it is also something that AI through case law analysis can do in the future without being done by humans. **The clock is ticking against the government and local governments, which are at the forefront of changing with the times. In a rapidly changing era, it is impossible**

to reform by focusing only on the opinions of the younger generation who are accustomed to the Fourth Industrial Revolution, but the main reason for MZ Jooul's resignation can be summarized as a reward and gratitude system that goes against human instinct. Still, it's a great place for our lazy brains to live in an environment where there is no risk of survival. Therefore, there is still a way to prove one's worth through loyalty and integrity to the organization. Now, no large company puts this value first and is not in line with the current times.

Sincerity is an evaluation received from others. If someone is rumored to be sincere, the value of that person does not at least not decrease. However, unless a system is introduced in which people with good problem-solving skills other than sincerity are valued more, it will be difficult to accept expertise and diversity through self-development, and it is easy for unproductive and repetitive work to become the main thing in a rapidly changing era. **The fact that civil servants have adopted the NCS and PSAT long after 2025, rather than focusing on memorization subjects, which was a test that lasted until 2024, can be seen as a sign that problem-solving skills are now more important than conscientiousness, and it also proves that civil servants are the slowest changing organizations.**

Of course, just because you're a private company doesn't mean it's easy to do a job evaluation. However, even if there is an error in the evaluation method, it differs from the civil servant in that there is a quick and appropriate compensation. This is because slaves who benefit the company by giving them salary incentives are designed by human instinct to live more as wage slaves. If large corporations were guaranteed the same compensation and retirement age as civil servants, which is the same socialist system, they would surely be in a league of their own. This happens because each person is in a different position, but at least this system does not fit with children who have experienced capitalist society in infinite competition since childhood. In other words, it is difficult for civil servants to satisfy various needs other than the need for survival in human instinct, and the more they do not develop their own characteristics, the more they are integrated, advantageous, and suitable for the group.

The reason why this phenomenon occurs in places where class society is clearly divided, such as civil servants, public enterprises, and the military, can be attributed to the influence of the messages that have been established in society from the past. There are six ways to be widely remembered by people (1. Simplicity 2. Surprises 3. Concreteness 4. Reliability 5. Emotion 6. Story) It can be expressed in a condensed way. Those who take advantage of the established message from society have excerpted one of the speeches of the President of the United States as a politician.

"The United States must be committed to one goal. So that within the next 10 years, we will be able to land a man on the lunar surface and return safely."

These messages have the following characteristics:

The content of the message is very simple and intrigues people. And whether the pledge is true or not, it is proven through arguments, giving people credibility. Lastly, use storytelling techniques that touch the heartstrings.

The more conservative the culture, the more emphasis is placed on simplicity among the six messages. Simplicity is a word that can be replaced by execution, and the simpler it is, the easier it is for people to adapt to their environment and the easier it is to remember. Steve Jobs and Zuckerberg are said to have emphasized to their employees the phrase "reduce, reduce, reduce" when starting and running a company. This phenomenon also applies to social culture, and is especially evident in conservative groups such as the military and civil servants. The simpler the command or directive, the more people remember the message. If you are a man in the Republic of Korea, you can understand why the military is so inefficient in its administrative processes. The civil service group also shows better administration than the military, but it is doggin' gaggin. **Replacing complexity with simplicity may be a high-level strategy, like politicians' messages, but it shows that the emphasis is on speed and execution rather than efficiency, imprinting the command or directive system more on employees. People with** a strong S tendency to MBTI, which is commonly known, are relatively simpler and more realistic than N, and they have their own routines. Among my friends, the children who come from military and civil service families are conscientious, have strong vitality, follow routines, and generally have strong execution skills. Because of the emphasis placed on simplicity among the messages established in society, this group suffers from many inefficient work processes in a passive position with no sense of agency.

Private companies, on the other hand, are not focused on simplicity, but rather as a group united by the purpose of benefiting the company, and they use all six messages. Since it is a profit-making group, it can be seen that private companies are better suited as the best strategy for enslaving people, similar to human instinct. Since civil servants work for the public interest, they work based on the principle of legal interpretation rather than flexibility, so they are bound to feel frustrated when they are viewed from the outside. **So they play their own league in a capitalist country based on the socialist system (conditions: equal compensation).**

1.2 Chickens in a Coop

'Chicken in a chicken coop' is a Korean proverb that can be interpreted in various ways depending on the situation, but in general, it is a proverb that figuratively expresses the interference of people within a group or organization with each other. The Republic of Korea is sandwiched between major powers (China and Japan) locally, and has entered the era of unlimited competition due to high population density and resource constraints in a small land mass. In the life of struggling to climb up by clawing at each other and trampling on someone, the chickens gradually go crazy and begin to have a vase that only the people of our country are there. Also, we live in a white apartment like a matchbox, and we look like chickens in a chicken coop.

However, just as the overall economic life (salary, assets, etc.) is determined by which country you are born in, it is actually a blessing to be born in our country. As the saying goes, if you were born as a citizen of the Republic of Korea, you can't be said to be very unlucky. The standard of living and economic power remain in the top 10, and at least the people do not starve to death because of food.

In the same way , **the world of civil servants is not starving to death at least. If you pass the civil service, it feels like moving out of the chicken coop and into a new chicken coop. If the previous chicken coop was a competition of crazy chickens who attacked each other and had to beat someone to get food, the chicken coop you moved in seems at first to be a little decent chicken coop where you can feed and raise chicks until you grow old. However, in this environment, the chickens begin to get sick rather than go crazy. Now that survival has been resolved, the ego wants to satisfy its higher needs, but as I said earlier, This organization is far from the desire for self-actualization.** Even the bold roosters lose their gender identity due to the meticulousness in the coop and the chicken coop culture that requires a keen view (a problem with civil service work, which will be discussed later).

Obtaining a job with a guaranteed retirement age through competition means that you have solved your need for survival, and to exaggerate it, it is also a life in which you have given up on self-development as a risk-free life. The human brain is lazy, and anyone is apt to become lazy in such an environment.

On the one hand, it is also the reason why men and women in jobs with guaranteed retirement age, such as civil servants and public companies, get married early and have children. Employees of civil servants and public enterprises who are guaranteed retirement age show figures that differ from the birth and marriage rate statistics released by the National Statistical Office. Female civil servants usually marry in their late 20s~early 30s, and many men also marry in their early 30s. It is a phenomenon that can only be seen in the city of civil servants. Stability gives them an advantage in marriage and child-rearing, but unfortunately, their next goal is to raise the next chick from the chickens in the coop. **They take the steps that society demands from them to college, employment, and marriage, and they are faithful to their desires, nothing more, nothing less.**

And when a child is born, it gives them the right to work for the child, so from then on, they live as a paycheck slave forever. Eight out of ten of the people I met said they wanted to leave their jobs, and most of the unmarried people said they didn't quit because they didn't know what they liked or what to do, and married people said they had no choice but to work for the sake of their families.

Satisfaction with this job also varies by gender. The hormone testosterone is also present in women, but it is a hormone that is secreted incomparably more in men. People who have actually achieved something or made a big deal use this hormone to become successful, and this hormone plays a big role in why there are so many successful people in the world.

I agree that gender equality should lead to equal rights, but the brains of men and women are so different.

The stronger the influence of testosterone, the more adventurous and thrilling men are. In addition, the left brain (the area of practice) is more developed than the right brain, and it has one-dimensional thinking. Women, on the other hand, are dominated by three hormones: estrogen, oxytocin (the hormone of empathy and love), and prolactin (a hormone related to milk and children), which is more like fantasy and enjoyment. The right side of the brain (the emotional area) is more developed, and they have complex thinking. Harmony and tradition (peace, empathy, caring, altruism) are important, and the propensity for practice, adventure, and pleasure (rebellion, independence, struggle, selfishness) is weaker than that of men. Therefore, women are more likely to seek a job with a guaranteed retirement age or stability. There are many people who want the gentle waves to come from their lives.

In addition, as the brain ages, the levels of hormones secreted are starkly different, unlike the brain in youth. Levels of dopamine and testosterone stimulation drop significantly, and the stress hormone cortisol increases. As a result, the realm of adventure, pleasure, and practice plummets, and men also seek stability from this point on.

Therefore, when analyzing the tasks and characteristics of the civil service job with hormones, it can be seen as the most unsuitable job for men in their 20s~30s who secrete heavy testosterone, and men in their 50s and above, who find it difficult to enjoy adventure and thrill after starting to age, begin to match the civil service model to some extent. And the most suitable model is that women who secrete estrogen and oxytocin have the highest emphasis on stability, so they are more satisfied with their jobs relative to men. Since women are stronger than men in harmony, tradition, peace, empathy, consideration, and altruism, it is advantageous for local governments and governments to entrust women with work, even if they are somewhat less effective than men.

If you join this organization in your 20s or 30s, you will see more of the sloppiness of men than the boldness of the men due to the nature of the civil service.

In other words, if a young rooster with strong testosterone enters the coop, it is likely to be spayed or neutered. If you are a male student in your 20s~30s, you need to reconsider this job.

1.3 Purpose of Existence

So, the majority of MZs who leave the civil service because it doesn't match their inclinations? Is it simply because the salary is low, as society sees it? Is that why you should leave the company? It may be a part of it, but it's not a major reason. So why are they quitting now?

Where was the goal of those who only studied for college entrance exams and then job hunting, as if they were printed in a factory, to become civil servants? My goal was to take the civil service exam and pass it, but there are few people who take on the challenge of thinking about how they will build their life journey and what kind of mindset they will have to become a member of society after becoming a civil servant. To be more specific, your goal and vision of becoming a civil servant is just because it's okay to get married, because it's a job that is appreciated to some extent, because you have a guaranteed retirement age, because you have a pension. Unlike a large company, you can retire, you don't have to pay results, and you can get around comfortably? I prepared with this in mind. **I'm just trying to pass the test, but I don't have a firm goal as to why I want to be a member of a civil service organization. If that happens, even if you pass the exam and become a civil servant, you will be confused about your existence.** In the first or second year, they are too busy adapting to society to think about it, but as the years of their tenure accumulate, they begin to cast philosophical doubts on themselves.

'What am I?' and 'What am I doing here?' 'If the problem of survival (if I have a lot of money) is solved, will I continue to go here?' 'What are my values?'

There are quite a lot of people who think about themselves through many experiences and challenges in their youth and twenties, and who are worried about their identity, which should be settled with their own values and philosophies, after they get a job at a company after they are over thirty. Of course, this is a phenomenon that not only civil servants but also office workers go through, but this is a place where people's instincts, desires, and the capitalist system are opposed, and their philosophical doubts are relatively steeper than those of those who work in private companies. **This is because unless the role and existence are higher than the head of the agency or the director, it is limited to satisfying the subordinate needs of human beings.** Even during his tenure, none of his colleagues or seniors could answer exactly why civil servants exist, and he lost his independence and did not know why he was doing his job. After that period, no one raises philosophical doubts and raison d'être.**That's why one of the most common things that civil servants say is, "After 10 years of work, it will be different."**

People are beings who live by prioritizing the needs of individuals, not organizations, and they are given responsibility for their work by focusing only on receiving a salary, which is the purpose of the individual. I don't care why this organization exists or exactly what it does. Human beings have both selfish and altruistic hearts, but the more a group emphasizes altruism and sacrifice without sufficient compensation, the easier it is to fall apart. **Unlike the civil servants of the past, we are a minority of people who choose careers as a matter of survival, so if the limits of self-growth and the reason for their existence are not suitable, they will leave.**

Just as people don't care about others, public officials can be seen as paying attention to others in the brains of those who question why this organization exists. So, is there anyone who has not yet experienced it who can tell you what a civil servant does?

The work of civil servants can be broadly divided into two parts: revitalization of the domestic economy and welfare.

There are many people who get a sense of accomplishment and pride by helping others, but unless they are in a situation where they can afford it psychologically or financially, it is difficult to move forward in the corporate life because it goes against human instinct if they only give responsibility in the spirit of public interest and service. Examinees say, "I will become a public servant for the development of the country, sacrifice for others, and live for the purpose of the public good rather than for my own personal interests!" If there is a crazy guy who says that, he will admit it, but most of the time he will find a reason to pass in his own interests.

In other words, it is difficult for a group or organization to take precedence over an individual, and this organization is a group that goes against human instinct and is made up for a public purpose. Since the examinees are golden spoons, if they have a lot of assets and power, they can be considered more suitable for civil servants. Since most of them are challenged by the children of the common people, **it is difficult to justify the raison d'être of individual civil servants as the cause of welfare and sacrifice of the public good.** The false direction of auditing, in which equal salaries and retirement age are guaranteed, with no rewards and reprimands are prioritized over praise, is also difficult to fit in with people living in capitalism.

Therefore, from a capitalist point of view, the reason for their existence can be the revitalization of the domestic economy. I think that the manufacturing conglomerates that produce through consumption abroad are more important for our country's position, but the domestic economy is just as important. However, since Korea is a country that has grown into an export-oriented economy centered on manufacturing, there is no justification for the existence of civil servants here. In order to revitalize the domestic economy, taxes are collected, SOC projects or welfare items are created to execute the budget, and in the process of execution, small and medium-sized enterprises, self-employed people, etc., exchange money with each other. However, they have a culture based on simplicity without individual identity, They turn into zombies that do as they are told, and in the end, they don't even know why they exist. **The pride that comes from helping others against human instinct is only a momentary**

feeling, but isn't there a precedent for a socialist country to live worse than a capitalist country? The reason why socialism has collapsed is because it has abandoned the basic human needs of greed and greed.

After all, the profession of civil servant is suitable for those above the upper middle class in the class of wealth, but it is an ironic profession in which they have no reason to prepare for this exam.

check point
(Absence of goals)

Write down why you want to be a civil servant right away.

When asked why they want to be rich, the answers of those who can't get rich are as follows.

"I want to live comfortably, because if I have money, I can do what I want. I want to leave a boring company," and so on, and he doesn't know why he wants to get rich. That's why it's hard for them to get rich. If you don't know why you want to become a civil servant, you'll lose your color and start living like a zombie in a boring and repetitive life.

After passing, you must have a sense of purpose in your life and a sub-specific goal according to your sense of purpose.

1-4 Domestic Economy

Domestic demand is an economy that is fueled by domestic consumption and investment, and is an economic activity driven by domestic consumption and production activities, such as consumer spending, business investment, and construction activities. When the domestic economy is strengthened, the domestic economic growth rate increases and job creation is stimulated. In order to promote domestic demand, it is necessary to stimulate consumption and increase investment by enterprises.

In order to achieve economic development and growth, the government's policy formulation and implementation should stimulate the activities of various economic actors, such as the production and investment of enterprises and the consumption of consumers. Although the process for economic development varies depending on the country's economic structure, industrial structure, and international economic environment, **the role of the government and local governments is quite important in strengthening Korea's domestic economy and developing the economy.** I think everyone feels what the current domestic economy is like in Korea. The money that was released countless times to revitalize the economy during the COVID-19 pandemic is being taken the lead by the United States through tapering or austerity. As a result, the U.S. took the big step of raising interest rates, and South Korea also raised interest rates several times in line with the U.S. to defend the exchange rate and prevent inflation. Of course, it cannot be said that the interest rate was raised only by the reversal of the interest rate differential with the United States, but even if you look at the inflation indicators, the base rate had to be raised. Consumers don't open their wallets easily. According to the 2023 KDI Economic Outlook Report, You can see the table below.

As such, the government and local governments need to create items that promote consumption. Therefore, the heads of local governments (elected politicians) who have a firm sense of purpose for reappointment based on elections and voting, use the strategy of using SOC projects in civil engineering or architecture, which is easy to call an achievement once it is completed, and temporarily increases job creation. However, unlike the head of an agency, the brains of lower-level officials execute the budget without having the independence of why, so people with strong curiosity and independence are likely to fall into despair. So, if you don't do your civil service work with the mindset of the head of an agency, it's easy to fall into oblivion to the point where you don't know why you're doing it.

Before describing the problems of democratically elected politicians in the future, let**'s first analyze the organization of the organization without experiencing both the position of the producer and the consumer, and the strategy is nominally based on desk administration, and the strategy of restricting the independence of the person in charge according to obedience to the instructions from the top usually results in a strategy that does not correspond to reality.** Most of us live the life of a consumer. Producers are usually entrepreneurs or people who make something on their own and sell their items to an unspecified number of people.

Although the government is a producer who stimulates consumption, most of the government officials are consumers who consume by receiving a salary. Therefore, if the goal is to revitalize the domestic economy, it is not only important to attract companies, but **if the economy is to be revived through budget execution, those who have worked as the brains of producers at least once should be free from the influence of democratically elected politicians to some extent and come up with diversified opinions and implement them. GNOME's swift execution has an impact on economic revitalization, but direction is more important than speed.**

In addition, it is difficult to feel pride as a public servant, and if you play a balance game about whether the domestic economy or the export economy is more important in the economic structure of the country, the people will say that it is the export economy.

So how are companies that work as producers, who create their own systems and strategies and sell them to an unspecified number of people, different from consumers?

Producers differ in how their brains work.

Chapter 2: The Mind of a Civil Servant vs. Entrepreneur

After much deliberation, I decided to leave the company, and it seemed to move intuitively. Actions took precedence over thoughts. While I was at work, I was devoting myself to creating a side income (pipeline), and even now, money is coming in as a side income. For nearly 8 months after leaving the company, I worked on the economic academy project and the carbon credit project, and failed.... It is over, and now it is re-envisioning a capital-free start-up.

The rich are on the right in the economic quadrant, and they are said to be building more than five pipelines.

During my tenure, I wanted to have a producer's brain from the perspective of a civil servant (worker), and I steadily built up additional income one by one to accommodate diversity in my brain. **By the time I was working on building the pipeline, I understood why people have to sell at least one item in their lives, and how the brains of producers and consumers are different.** Producers are constantly on a journey to discover themselves anew in different environments, but consumers make passive choices within the system created by the producers. The biggest difference was the subjectivity based on self-identity. For those who are thinking about quitting, I recommend that they at least develop the ability to sell something before leaving.

The Producer's Brain

Producers primarily produce and deliver products or services, and they often value creativity, problem-solving, and execution. Producers have a variety of responsibilities, such as running a business or managing the manufacturing process. Therefore, the producer's brain values the ability to develop and execute innovative and creative ideas. Producers are also interested in gaining a competitive edge in order to bring their products or services to market and sell them successfully.

This can help them develop marketing strategies and awareness of market trends to stay competitive.

The Brain of the Consumer (Mostly Workers)

Consumers are mainly towards the side of purchasing and using products or services in the market. They mainly focus on choices, value judgments, and satisfaction. Collect and compare information to choose from a variety of products or services that meet your needs and preferences. Therefore, consumers' brains tend to develop judgment and decision-making skills, and they value the satisfaction they get from using a product or service. Thus, consumers' brains can shape their perceptions of rewards and satisfaction from their choices or purchases. Most of us go through life as consumers. They buy products made by others through their salaries and live with satisfaction. Public servants are supposed to work from the point of view of producers, which is to collect taxes from the people and stimulate the domestic economy, but the reason why it is difficult to work from the perspective of producers is that it is difficult to match the purpose of the individual because the business is carried out with taxes. Running a business with someone else's money and not your own is a separate thing from your personal purpose. If the business costs their own money and not taxes, they will keep the lights on and hang day and night to make a profit. In order to prevent laziness rather than one's own choice, the person often goes back and forth from one department to another with a single personnel appointment paper, making it even more difficult to work with a sense of responsibility. Frequent department changes also reflect the lack of professionalism in the organization.

If you're in a civil service organization that doesn't appreciate diversity, your brain will become passive here. Instinctively, we have sexual intercourse with someone other than our relatives and have children. This is to compensate for the genes that are lacking in oneself and to pass on a better inheritance to the second generation. Diversity is a great word with relative complements such as immunity to disease, intelligence, talent, and appearance. However, if you look at the reports written by civil servants, they have their own certain framework, and if you deviate from that framework, it is easy to be stigmatized. **At most, there are 5 people who have the authority to approve the civil servants' reports, and if there are few, it ends with the team leader and the section chief. In order to satisfy 3~5 consumers, a report with low execution and high planning is written according to the taste of the approving authority.** Of course, writing down the goals from top to bottom in detail on how to execute the budget given in the report is a great help in setting the direction, but it can be seen that there is a great lack of execution due to lack of expertise. If you are in an administrative position, it is difficult to say that you have expertise because most of the interpretation is in accordance with the law, but if you are in a technical position, there are many tasks that require expertise. Since the technical service and construction company are selected and ordered, the variables that occur according to the execution will be done by the contractor and the contractor, which are the bidding companies.

In other words, the brains of people who write reports on how to plan a business, rather than direct execution, are relatively difficult to develop. Even the words and word order used in the report are similar to everyone, so a brain that doesn't recognize diversity won't realize exactly five years from now what kind of environment it's working in. To give another example, it is difficult for a local government to operate on a municipal basis, so those who receive government funds from the country receive extra points or have an advantage in promotion. Again, I don't know what kind of creative idea was used to get the budget from the government, but it is only a report with a plan, and the most important area of implementation is missing.

So how are entrepreneurs' brains different?

In order to improve their ability to execute, entrepreneurs also set detailed and specific goals from the top, middle, and lower levels to achieve small goals one by one. However, the biggest difference, as I said earlier, is in the area of execution. As soon as a goal is set, entrepreneurs move forward with feedback through execution. Every entrepreneur knows that goal setting is concise and that execution can change course and even change goals. 3~5 approving people do not use their own system, and many people from unspecified capitalist markets are customers. How to plan and market it, how much money will it cost, etc. **The difference in subjectivity can be said to be enormous due to the influence of the brain over time.**

The more years you have been in the civil service, the more convinced you are that you become a person who can't do anything outside. For them, the idea of retiring and getting a pension is true. Society is making people who don't know what kind of system to design and implement. They usually **focus on form and procedure rather than content, which is quite different from the feeling of looking at things carefully and carefully.** Depth of thought can increase the ability to make effective decisions, but it is a well-known fact that thinking alone does not teach action, and organizations that do not appreciate diversity are more decadent. **These small differences make it impossible for ordinary public servants, with the exception of elected officials (politicians) and their staffs, to rise to the top of the hierarchy of wealth under capitalism.**

2-1 Lack of Reward / Dopamine Slave to the Smartphone

In addition to testosterone, a hormone that is deeply related to the organization of civil servants is dopamine, the receptors of which vary depending on the person's innate temperament. A friend from high school of mine who feels happy with a little dopamine.

When this friend orders chicken after work, he just smiles and is happy. On the other hand, people with large dopamine receptors are willing to put geeky ideas into practice and continue to want bigger and stronger stimulation. On the negative side, they may have broken dopamine receptors, or they may be born with large receptors in their temperament, but the brains of modern people are not satisfied with most of the dopamine levels due to the well-known effects of smartphones and social media.

MZ, who is accustomed to smartphones and social media, which are the products of geniuses who reversely exploit the psychology of ordinary people, will have problems if there is no immediate compensation. In fact, in order to enjoy greater rewards and thrills, you have to have endless patience and not rush for rewards in front of you, but the younger generation has grown up in a system where immediate rewards are given. A temporary way to stop younger generations from leaving the workforce is to quickly compensate them with a variety of dopamine patterns that are appropriate for them, but this is not feasible and desirable. Of course, there are certainly problems because it is a system in which civil servants are not rewarded and have a strong sense of responsibility, but it is also a problem that the younger generation needs to improve.

If you read the book "Instabrain", you will find that the brain, which has been handed down from primitive times, has not yet adapted to the modern era.

MZ, who grew up in the modern era, can quench his hunger by opening the refrigerator, and if he is curious, he can open his smartphone and immediately satisfy his intellectual desires. In addition, they have clearly learned their position and rank by comparing themselves with others through social media, and they are a generation that knows very well that it is difficult to rise to the upper ranks even if they try. One example of a reason for not getting married is that men find it easier to satisfy their sexual desires. Since it can be resolved immediately without meeting a woman, it is easier to be alone than to adjust with consideration and empathy, unlike my parents' generation. After the age of 30, when sex hormones decrease even more, there are many people who choose to take up hobbies alone.

In this generation, even rewards for promotion don't have much of a dopamine effect. **To be clear, MZ civil servants have no desire to be promoted. Since** the benefits of being promoted are small compared to the effort, he manages to work in a comfortable department and then arrives home to enjoy his evening life. **Public employee unions and non-civil servants consider salary to be the primary reason for MZ's departure, but it is by no means the reason for their departure.** The salary, which served as compensation, was a drug for the older generation, but the MZ civil servants came in knowing that the salary was low, so it is not a consideration in the first place. In other words, you need to reward them with something other than promotion and money. Just as you have to give what the other person wants in a relationship to be in a relationship, the younger generation will go on if you give them the rewards they want right away. We need to keep trying new ways to do this, such as fostering a sense of identity for why they work here and creating a sense of pride in providing administrative processes and services to citizens.

On the other hand, here are some examples of compensation used by private companies: It's a common rule in self-help books, and it's well-known to everyone these days.

1.80% people are limited to what 20% people produce and own. (The 80:20 rule)

2. The shorter the deadline for a task or the act of producing, the more focused and efficient the brain will be. (Parkinson's Law)

The 80/20 rule is easy to understand.

I've always wondered who owns so many buildings around me. If you ask your friends, no one has a landlord, but there are so many buildings. Now I know. Most of Seoul's upper class, or 20 percent, own buildings.

Most theories in the world are divided into 80/20 rule. That means that 80% of the work I do in the company for 8 hours is useless. They know this and innovatively guarantee autonomous commuting time to young MZs, and even give them the autonomy to sit where they want according to the time they go to work, such as in a university library, rather than a fixed seat, because their brains are developed in various environments.

And Parkinson's Law is something that everyone in the workplace can relate to.

In the workplace, there is a secretary or bookkeeper who collects and submits documents. If you ask the secretary to send the files to your team by the next week, the team member prioritizes his or her work and ignores it for now. Instinctively, the team knows. When the deadline came, the secretary would submit the documents he was asked to submit with high efficiency. In other words, if they want to get a submission from a team member quickly, they can give them a very short deadline. However, with the exception of general affairs, the brains of the rest of the person are under negative stress as their thinking shifts from what they have to do **to what they can do.It's also Parkinson's Law that we can do in two hours at the speed of light what would take us eight hours to do before a vacation.**

The brain is an entity that makes it difficult to concentrate even for four hours a day. Most business departments and planning departments, except for dealing with civil affairs, can handle all of them if they work according to a specific plan with high efficiency for only 4 hours. **Putting the two together, the method of immediate compensation limits the important work to only the work that needs to be done, and gives them a certain degree of autonomy and independence by guaranteeing them a voluntary commute system or early departure rather than nominal flexible work by advancing the deadline.** However, since civil servants are a group that works for the public good, the repercussions that leaving work early will cause in the media are enormous. This is because incidents such as the death of a sincere Gimpo city official who was actually present outside of working hours but were judged not to be present based on speculation are still common in Korea. **I think everyone in the workplace knows how long a 52-hour period puts a strain on the brain and how inefficient and unnecessary practices we do in our company to fill those 52 hours.** However, you should also know MZ. Rather than the dopamine reward that is urgent in front of you, you should have a long-term perspective and persever, even if you don't want to do it, so you will get a greater reward. As you work, you may come up with your own unique items, so you need to develop the ability to endure and persevere.**You can leave after one or two years and become better, but no organization is ideal. I** wrote this because the union or the head of an agency that wants to reform the civil service organization may not really know the reason for MZ's departure. And even if they know the actual problem, since what they do in a formal way (showing) is their job, **it is a waste of budget to order an organizational culture improvement service rather than a practical alternative to prevent resignation, so I wrote this chapter.**

2.2 Inefficiencies and Unnecessary Practices

Unnecessary paperwork and procedures

Often, you have to follow unnecessary paperwork and procedures. This slows down the pace of high-priority unique work. There are countless materials that need to be submitted to the secretary of the department as requested by other departments, and simple materials such as weekly meeting materials and audit materials must be prepared one by one. In addition, if you are a local government, you will receive numerous official letters that you have to submit to the government department, which is a higher authority. I'm still wondering, 'Do humans have to do this themselves?' There are so many simple summations that I think. I have a lot to say about writing a report, so I'll make a separate chapter to talk about it.

Excessive meetings and meeting culture

There are times when there is an excessive number of meetings where the purpose is not clear. This wastes time and hinders actual work. When you have a meeting, do problem-solving ideas come from your brain? When I was working in the Urban Development Department of the City Hall, the average number of meetings I had was close to 3~5 a day. There were many meetings in the morning, such as LH and Urban Development Corporation, engineering firms, team meetings, and department meetings in the afternoon, but when they did meet each other, they were more like delivering information than discussing solutions to project promotion problems. And at the end of the meeting, when I was working or bruising ~ slapping, I thought, 'What if I did this?, Why don't I do that?' The brain offers me a new alternative. Like me, the brains of the people in charge of other organizations discussed the problems of business promotion with each other over the phone or KakaoTalk and sought solutions during non-meeting times.

In a meeting, the brain is in a state of tension and it is difficult to find a way to solve a problem. The reason for this is that the meetings themselves are overly structured and stressful, and there is no room for creative and free thinking in this environment. Meetings usually play a big role in providing information to the person in charge or showing the boss how the person in charge is working.

Inefficient decision-making process

Decision-making processes are often complex and inefficient. What's really annoying is that if the mindset of the team leader and the manager don't coincide and they disagree, they will keep retrieving the document when they are in charge of approval. I would rather understand if it was a flag fight, but people have different perspectives depending on their inclinations. So, if I post a report as I insisted, the team leader says that it should be changed like this, so I change it, and if I change it to the taste of the team leader, the manager asks me why I did this again and asks me to take it back. It would be great if the two of you could agree and inform us when drafting and approving the report, but it seems that this is what I have done throughout my tenure. In addition, even if there is a person with full authority, if the mind of the boss above the person with full authority (the commissioner or the mayor) is not known, the decision will be delayed. If you work in a ward that is smaller than a city, the opinion of the person with full authority does not matter. The smaller the institution, the more the head of the institution (the mayor of the ward) has more control over it.

Incompetent distribution of work and resource management

Tasks are not evenly distributed, and resources are not managed efficiently. Here, if you do a good job, they give you more work. And the more you work, the more likely you are to be grateful. The funny thing is that there was a person who didn't work for two whole years, but he was always able to get a free pass in the auditor general audit or the joint government audit. The strange audit system that rewards and punishes people for their work will also be detailed later. And as you know if you are an office worker, there are many people who are promoted by word of mouth rather than by work. I thought that in-house politics, which is a blow-up in social life, was also a unique ability of that person, and I thought that winning people's hearts was a better ability than my work ability, so I was not dissatisfied. However, there are many people who work with their mouths and do not work, so there is always a phenomenon where work is pulled to one side. Of course, as I said earlier, those who have an audit free pass don't work with their mouths, and they don't do their work.

Stagnant Organizational Culture and Resistance

There is a high level of resistance to new ideas or changes. As you know, creativity and innovation in the work of the civil service are not enough. As I will tell you in a later chapter, depending on whether you are from Koshi or Vigo, you will have the opportunity to do creative work. If I meet with the director from the city of Vigo, I will start by analyzing whether there are such cases in other cities.

As everyone knows, it is a practice that not only civil servants but all office workers often encounter. However, one thing that is a little different from a large company is that it has a team. Having been to both places, the word team means different things. Large companies set a single goal, and the roles of team members are distributed. Therefore, even if you are scolded more by your seniors, it is easier for you to learn the work and professionalism. And since they run under the same goal of the company's profits, they tend to trust and rely on each other. Of course, it was a headache to compete with other teams. However, civil servants are nominally present not as a team to run towards a single goal. Each person in charge has its own Because of their work, even if they are on the same team, they work alone with different organizations. Every team member's job is different, and it's not even relevant. Even the army has the concept of a reserve gunner and a gunner ...As a result, new employees often learn to do their work and are in charge of their work alone with nowhere to turn to anyone. **It is also true that young civil servants find it difficult to respond to complaints, and there are many suicides and resignations.**

2.3 Influence of Elected Officials

The people who are affected by elections more than the citizens are the public servants. Since the budget is executed under the influence of elected politicians, it means that the company has changed ownership. In this situation, if the political party changes, many of the things that have been carried out so far will change, and the director-level staff, which is a group of high-ranking civil servants, will be replaced. **So what is the impact on lower-level officials?**

Influence is applied differently depending on the agency, but when the head of the agency changes, lower-level officials are also subject to restrictions such as promotions, vacations, and in-house benefits. And the smaller the institution (ward office), the less TO be promoted, so it is more influenced by personnel authority than the city officials, who have a relatively large number of TOs.

The examinees passed the test in the same city, but depending on whether they are assigned to the city or the ward, the promotion and welfare benefits are slightly different. It is only within the city, but it can be regarded as an independent institution in terms of the concept of an autonomous district, and even though the city hall is a higher institution than the ward office, the mayor and the mayor often fight each other. This doesn't happen very often, because the borough's budget is small, but you can't get city subsidies, so you don't have a bullet to make the mayor's promises. **And if such a flag fight breaks out, the mayor may stop interacting with the borough, so the people who suffer the most are the lower-level officials. If** we are going to push forward with the intention of not receiving city subsidies, it can be said that the authority of the head of the borough, which is an independent agency, plays a bigger role than we think. Therefore, the speed of promotion of civil servants varies greatly depending on their luck rather than their ability, such as where they work or where they are located. Civil servants who do not have a job go down to the ward office after taking the city's transfer test, which has a relatively high number of TOs, and then go back down to the ward office, and those who are on the political line do not need to take the transfer test to the city because the ward mayor will promote them within their term. And they can be promoted faster than city officials. Of course, it is best if there is a dense city It's good, and in this case, even if you get promoted in the city, you don't go down to the ward, so you continue to have a promotion advantage over others. **Thus, depending on which party's elected politician comes, it will have a great impact on the promotion that they prioritize in the lower ranks.**

In addition, democratically elected politicians seek to protect the interests of certain parties in their constituencies. This can have the negative effect of prioritizing the interests of a particular group over the interests of the nation as a whole. One way to prioritize the interests of a particular group is to boost the projects of the people involved (camps) after being elected, and as a method, the order of the head of the agency comes to the ears of the person in charge without knowing it, mainly through voluntary contracts (up to 22 million won including VAT). (If you are a female business, you can sign a contract of up to 30 million won, so many business owners usually do business in the name of their wives.)

I understand the intention to take care of the people who helped him in the election, but the responsibility for the ordering lies with the lower-level civil servant who is in charge. This could later be disciplined by an audit and hinder promotion. Of course, the person in charge has the right to choose. There are those in charge who go ahead with their convictions even when there is pressure, and there are those in charge who sign a contract with the company because they think it's a good thing. However, no matter what choice you make, there are bound to be problems later.

The person in charge who works with the dog pair and the other way is not in the eyes of the head of the agency, who has the authority over personnel, or is at a disadvantage to reputation or promotion. In addition, the person in charge who made the contract with the company desired by the head of the agency may also be caught in the audit and disciplined. Therefore, if the head of an institution is willing to take care of the person in charge of his order, rather than just using him, he will often be promoted before the audit of the higher authority arrives. If you get promoted, even if you are disciplined, it will take a long time for you to be promoted to the next level, so even if you are disciplined now, there is no problem at all until your turn for the next promotion. However, if the head of the agency does not take care of you even though you have pushed him with a voluntary contract, you may suffer more damage than the person who acted with confidence. Of course, the amount of the voluntary contract is so small that it is usually carried out by the ward, and since the city has a relatively large budget, it is possible to push it with various expedients by avoiding the bidding method in the national market, such as materials and goods other than construction, within a reasonable range, rather than pushing it with a voluntary contract. Of course, large-scale SOC projects with a very large amount of money can only be carried out through bidding.

Then there are the local events that the citizens enjoy. Some events are organized by the city, while others are organized by the city. Local events to meet with local leaders and manage their fields are too important for them, but they can only be re-elected if they keep their political promises, so the smaller the institution, the more cautious they are with their budgets. This means that you don't have a lot of budget to take care of both. As a result, politicians often fill local events with the manpower and labor of public servants. Compared to using services, labor costs are overwhelmingly low, and the justification of an event for citizens is clear, so it is suitable for low-level officials. **That is why low-level officials are forced to go to work for politicians even on weekends and help with local events. From the**

food and songs that are indispensable to the event, they become waiters who deliver food or police officers who control traffic. Semi-compulsory participation in line with politicians' whims is one of the most stressful factors for lower-level officials. Of course, a city with a relatively larger budget than a borough uses professional services to host events and improves quality. As a civil servant, it can be said that in terms of emergency work, local events, and welfare, city officials are freer than municipal officials.

Another thing that affects lower-level officials is that when the head of an agency changes, work on long-term projects that were previously done is stopped. Newly elected politicians focus on short-term strategies in order to be re-elected in the next election. Therefore, the lower-level civil servants in charge of fulfilling the pledges are entrusted with the commitments of the new democratically elected politicians in the existing projects. Civil servants move and move departments with pieces of paper, which they call items, and the time when the paper pieces show the most power is when the head of the agency changes. Low-level civil servants are also less common than high-ranking officials, but there are a large number of personnel appointments, resulting in the transfer of departments and reorganization.

Lastly, if you are a local government official, there are ward councilors and city councilors who you often meet. During my tenure, I had a lot of questions about their existence. I understand that their job is to represent the citizens and monitor the efficient use of local government budgets, but the audit of the councillors is more politically influential, so they are politicians who work to act as a check on the head of a political party and to manage the votes of the constituencies (the interests of the constituencies) or the votes of the members of the National Assembly. Since it is a group driven by certain interests, it is not clear whether it has a positive effect on the development of the civil service organization, **and various pressures and vague orders come in even to lower-level civil servants.**

That's why officials are so cautious about voting.

2.4 The Need for AI Adoption

When the stock prices of Maso, NVIDIA, Google (Alphabet), related ETFs related to the Fourth Industrial Revolution and AI, QQQ (technology stocks), and SOXX Semiconductor reached new highs, articles related to AI, one of the Fourth Industrial Revolutions, began to pour in in Korea as well. I was curious about what kind of future would unfold in the future, so I bought and read KAIST Future Strategy 2022, and Apple and Tesla companies, which I saw through a friend in Silicon Valley in the United States after leaving the company, were already introducing AI. Jeremy Rifkin, an American economist and futurist, suggested that the advancement of AI will bring the end of human labor. The liberation of human beings from labor is not a positive aspect, but a negative one. It means the loss of jobs, and the idea of robots and machines replacing human jobs is becoming inevitable. **The above is a topic on which futurists are divided on whether or not to give AI robots autonomous will. If there is no actual autonomous will, there are many sayings circulating in the world that humans will eventually become the main actors in monitoring AI, and that AI will eventually dominate humans.**

So, what would happen if AI was introduced to the civil service population?

The civil service organization is largely divided into three departments: the planning department, the business department, and the welfare department, and the rest of the departments, except for the welfare department, think that it is easy to adopt AI. You may think of the planning department as a place where creative ideas are poured out, but since it is a **department that embodies and implements the promises of elected politicians, I think that AI analysis is more reliable, not people, who judge the likelihood of the success of politicians' promises. However, while AI analytics can help us achieve better outcomes, we believe it requires human competence**

and judgment. This is called cognitive labor, and as human beings are given autonomy, they become responsible. If AI has autonomy, then it has the same responsibilities. **Therefore, legal penalties for AI must also be created, which raises complex issues. Therefore, I think it is difficult for AI to replace human cognitive labor.**

Business departments can analyze business feasibility using AI and help the person in charge to handle legal and administrative procedures according to business procedures. Even now, in the case of large-scale SOC projects such as urban development projects, AI quickly judges and models the profit according to the sales rate. Until now, it has taken a long time to conduct a feasibility study of the project, but I think that the more advanced AI becomes, the faster the project starts, but also the shorter the time. And the best use of AI can build a defense against the complaints faced by many lower-level officials. There are various ways to use artificial intelligence (AI) to deal with civil complaints in the future, as follows.

Automated response system: It can provide basic answers to routine and repetitive complaints immediately. Through this, general and simple complaints are handled automatically, and civil servants can concentrate on their work.

Natural language processing technology: The contents of complaints can be analyzed using natural language processing technology and the main contents can be extracted. This allows officials to quickly identify the needs of the complainant and the gist of the complaint, and help them make a decision.

Prediction of problems through data analysis: By analyzing civil complaint data when related projects were carried out in the past, it is possible to predict areas or areas where problems are likely to occur, create a civil complaint response manual, and prepare in advance.

Personalized service provision: By analyzing the records and information of citizens who have filed complaints in the past and notifying public officials, it is possible to provide personalized services that are differentiated for each complainant. This ensures that citizens receive accurate answers.

Even now, with the development of computers and smartphones, unlike in the past, anyone who goes to the Ministry of Legislation can see the law. An analysis of judicial precedents in accordance with the law is also provided. In the future, I think there will be a world where AI will inform you of relevant laws, enforcement ordinances, and enforcement rules on your own, rather than citizens and public officials entering the legislative office. **Therefore, complaints about simple legal inquiries can be resolved sufficiently, and it is highly likely that the person in charge will only be responsible for cognitive labor according to the interpretation of the law. In addition, AI can quickly grasp the gist of the complainant's question and deliver it to the person in charge, and AI can also provide accurate answers with personalized services for each complainant.** There are many people who are forced to submit complaints that are against the law and ask for them to resolve them immediately, but I think that if AI responds to them with case law analysis data and a response system that says it is legally impossible **, it will not only reduce the number of emotions between human beings, but also reduce the number of public servants who suffer from malicious complaints.**

Lastly, simple aggregation, which is an inefficient task that accounts for 50% of the work of civil servants, can be resolved without issuing official notices to each ministry or department.

Chapter 3: Human Instincts and Desires

Let's analyze the organization of the civil service with human instinct. **Maslow's needs, as they are commonly known, can be categorized into five types: physiological needs, safety needs, love and belonging, respect needs, and self-actualization needs.**

Changes in the popularity of civil servants are highly relevant to the growth rate of the economy in our country. In the past, in an environment where it was difficult to survive, there would have been many people who wanted to become civil servants because of their physiological needs and their need for stability. It is also true that when the economy of the Republic of Korea grew remarkably from the era in which survival was important to the past, people with relatively low education or uneducated people chose to work as civil servants. Then, due to the foreign exchange crisis, the IMF was created, and the popularity of civil servants soared, and their popularity has continued to some extent to this day.

Currently, the GDP growth rate of developed countries in Western Europe and Japan, except for the United States, which ranks first in the world, is declining sharply, and Korea is going through the same procedure. **Without any special resources, the country has generated rapid economic growth through the manufacturing industry dominated by large corporations, thanks to human labor, the controversial Korea-Japan Agreement (known as black money / independence celebration money in Japan) during the Park Chung-hee regime, the special economy caused by the dispatch of troops to Vietnam, and the boom of the third base during the Chun Doo-hwan regime. And, like other advanced countries, it has entered an era of unlimited competition with each other as it faces the limit of GDP growth.** In the era of infinite competition, where people had to trample on each other to go up, they inherited even the shortcomings of Confucianism, which is characteristic of Eastern countries, and began to rank each other and check and compare their position with others according to their rank. And as time passed, with the advent of smartphones and the development of social media, it was now possible to know one's exact rank and position, and as a result, **MZ considered the instinct to maintain his reputation more important than anyone else. In primitive times, there were only about 30 individuals living in groups, but now they have to compete endlessly with others through social media. The number of individuals comparing with each other reaches hundreds of millions, There will always be people who are better than you, so you start to live with the consciousness of others' eyes rather than your own identity.**

Even if they only work part-time, there is no immediate problem with their livelihood (the desire for survival) and their parents' generation (vested interests) Since there are so many middle- and upper-middle-class people, the instinct to maintain the reputation of others was more important than the money when choosing a job. As the popularity of stable jobs with excellent work-life balance in the media and on the Internet increased, they began to prepare for it. Of course, it is true that people with excellent academic background and a head for studying preferred professional jobs to 9th and 7th grades, but **it is highly likely that the rest of the college graduates chose the civil service as a profession that was at least not attractive to others.**

Even now, even though the economy is said to be in difficulty due to the slump in domestic demand after COVID-19, it is a country that has been recognized as a developed country outside of a developing country. MZ young people don't have to starve to death right away even if they only work part-time. Japan, which took advantage of this and got ahead of us, is suffering from young whites, hikikomori, and freeters, and we are following Japan. **The reasons for the decline in the marriage rate and birth rate in Korea can be seen in the same vein as the development of technology, the division of seniority, which**

is common in Eastern countries, and the abandonment of marriage by young men due to the entry of women into society. I think that the problem of marriage information companies that classify people to arrange blind dates and promote them through the media also plays a role, but this is also a human instinct, so it cannot be helped.

In any case, MZ examinees who lived in the age of information flood could never have known about the salaries of civil servants. (If you don't know, you can search the salary list of civil servants on the Internet, because there are many additional benefits in addition to the basic salary, so if you just look at the basic salary table, there is a lot of difference from the annual salary, and if it is a local job, the salary varies depending on where you work. However, I think it is also true to some extent that due to COVID-19, this profession has also become less popular in terms of salary. **It's also true that the corona economy and the presidential election overlapped, and a lot of money was released, and the wage gap between public companies and large corporations widened due to inflation due to the inflation rate.... Before leaving the company, I worked for a major public company, and my girlfriend of 3 years of acting was 6 years younger, and her monthly salary was similar to that of me, who was 12 years of salary No. 10 (military experience, recognition of large company experience) ...Of course, the salaried people are there.**

In any case, since they know their salary, they prepare for the exam with a need **for safety, a need for respect, a need for belonging, and an instinct to maintain their reputation, rather than a survival need for immediate livelihood.** It is said that a new paradigm began with the emergence of NEETs, white beasts, and hikikomori in the past few years, but the rest of the MZ, who had tried to maintain their reputation instincts, began to face the reality after becoming public servants.

The need for security has been satisfied by the guaranteed retirement age, but the desire to be respected (depending on the views and preferences of public servants) will be shaken by the public's buzz, and finally, the desire for self-actualization at the highest level will be difficult to exercise in this group. **At present, even job seekers have been exposed to the MZ Juul resignation through various media, and the preference for civil servants is fading even faster. Now, job seekers have begun to prefer large corporations with high salaries and public companies called God's Workplace, and this is perhaps a visible process. There was also a bit of over-packaging of the civil service job in the media.**

However, I think that the profession of civil servant will become more popular again depending on the economy. The only profession that legally guarantees the retirement age is the civil service. If the economy slumps as severely as the IMF, the popularity of civil servants will rise, and won't the children who grew up without independence due to the indoctrination of the Republic of Korea look at the civil service as an enviable profession again because the instinct to maintain their reputation is more important than their own self-identity? And as soon as the coveted job becomes one's own, won't the lower needs be satisfied, and the higher needs of self-actualization cause resignations? Just as economic cycles repeat themselves and fashion comes and goes, this job is likely to do the same. **Of course, it is a very wrong phenomenon to prefer a job from the point of view of others without independence.**

Anyway, if we analyze it from human instinct, we think that it is civil servants > public companies > large corporations > small and medium-sized enterprises that have the potential to grow to satisfy their self-realization needs, so the **departure of MZ civil servants with high general intelligence will continue for the time being. This is because the civil service organization has lost its reputation instinct and is unable to satisfy even the needs of higher human beings.**

3.1 Are There Privileged Civil Servants?

Everyone knows the phenomenon of the rich and the poor due to wealth inequality, which is a problem of capitalism that is taught in social studies subjects from elementary school, and as a result, Germany, among the Germans, British, and French countries in Western Europe, which ranks high in the country's economic power, adopted revisionist capitalism in the 1970s. Revisionist capitalism in Germany is also called a "social market economy" and refers to the active intervention of the government for the welfare of the people while ensuring free competition in the market. The government shall create a fair environment of competition and implement policies to protect the socially disadvantaged.

On the other hand, capitalism in South Korea is based on the principle of a free market economy, and government intervention should be minimized. However, when an economic crisis or social problem occurs, I think it is necessary for the government to intervene temporarily to solve the problem.

In conclusion, German revisionist capitalism and South Korean capitalism have different philosophies and principles, but they both have in common the pursuit of people's welfare and economic growth. However, since the 21st century, there has been an argument that Germany should move from revisionist capitalism to neo-capitalism, which requires a reduction in government intervention and a return to a concept closer to the free market.

Revisionist capitalism was possible in Germany because it was a developed country with the fourth largest GDP. Of course, Germany is also a war criminal country, and after losing World War II, it suffered from national reparations and its economy suffered hyperinflation, and it became a developed country by profiting from the euro and marks (a beneficiary country of the European Union) from exports, but there is a big difference between the economic power of Germany and the Republic of Korea.

Typical indicators of economic strength include GDP (gross domestic product), GDP per capita, economic growth rate, and exports.

As of 2023, Germany's GDP is about $4,722.1 billion, ranking fourth in the world, while South Korea's GDP is about $1,701.4 billion, ranking 10th in the world. GDP per capita As of 2023, Germany's GDP per capita is about $45,800, ranking 24th in the world, while South Korea's GDP per capita is about $32,300, ranking 29th in the world. Germany's economic growth rate in 2024 is expected to be 0.2 percent, while South Korea's is expected to grow by 2.5 percent. Exports As of 2023, Germany's exports are about $1.74 trillion, ranking third in the world, while South Korea's exports are about $690 billion, ranking eighth in the world.

Have you ever heard the exaggerated statement that 'even the homeless wear luxury clothes in Germany'? European countries that were less fortunate than Germany emigrated to Germany for German citizenship and permanent residency, and the German government imposed strict immigration restrictions like the United States. As such, they tried to solve the problem of the rich and poor by massively organizing a welfare budget through government intervention, but the reason why they called for a return to the neo-capitalist system was because they went against human instinct.The vested class (the upper class) is positioned as the upper class of society, and they do their best to protect their assets, so even if those at the bottom of the wealthy class enjoy welfare benefits due to the intervention of the state and the government, the vested interests are bound to win in the end.

Before talking about the ninth-grade civil servants, Benz Ta mentioned the German revisionist capitalist system and the neo-capitalist system, which are different from those of the Republic of Korea, in order to show that the circumstances of each

new employee who passed the civil service examination are **different.** Some people need money right away to make ends meet, while others have wealthy parents who just go to work. **In other words, this is also a place where the phenomenon of rich and poor due to wealth inequality is greatly affected.**

Q: Then, what kind of environment is suitable for a civil service workplace?

A: **Paradoxically, golden spoons are the most suitable for civil servants.**

It's a heartbreaking story, but MZ believes that his life is determined by his parents' background, his abilities, and the umbilical cord that he is the best of the strings, according to the theory that the cutlery class theory was born and dominated the media. According to the cutlery class theory shown by the media, there are more new level 9 civil servants who meet the criteria for gold spoons than you might think. Of course, the standard of the golden spoon shown in the media is about the top 3% according to the class of the wealth of the Republic of Korea. As of 2023, it is estimated that the top 1% of households have a net worth of more than 2.9 billion, and even if the difference in assets from 1% ~ 0.1% is staggering, it means that there are quite a few public servants in the top 3% (net worth of 2 billion). **Even if you go to the underground parking lot of the city hall, it seems that there are more foreign cars than domestic cars, such as Mercedes, Audi, Volkswagen, and BMW, that are ridden by new graduates of the ninth grade. Nowadays, they drive foreign cars without their bosses noticing, so I was able to get to know their wealth even more.** However, I don't think there is a true gold spoon because the standards of gold spoons that I think of and the gold spoons that the media talk about are different. By my standards, many people with golden spoons are not able to design their lives however they want. They have no choice of profession because they have to take over the family business from birth, and they have to go to a prescribed school (study abroad) even in the process of growing up. There are not 100% of these people in the civil service organization. And to be honest, if you are a family with a net worth of 3 billion, I don't think the lifestyle and radius of life are much different. I think that from a net worth of more than 5 billion, they live a little differently than ordinary people.

I diverted for a moment, but as I said earlier, the standard of living due to the inequality of wealth divided according to the ability of the parents is enormous. Of course, it may be inaccurate because the sample is judged only by the metropolitan city where I have worked for 8 years, **but it is true that there are more 9th-grade gold spoons than I thought.**

So why are civil service gold spoons more suitable?

If you come to this organizational culture, there is a high probability that you will not be able to live a good life after marriage unless your parents' financial resources support you. **Most of the civil servants with a silver spoon or above have a house and cash on their parents when they get married, so there is a gap between them and the civil servants below the same spoon who start with a loan. According to current interest rates, even if you are a double earner, you will not be able to pay off your loans until you are 55 years old, so wealth inequality accelerates from the beginning.** So, according to the theory of the cutlery class, unless you are a gold spoon, even if you realistically earn a double income, you think that your salary is not enough to take out a house loan and raise a child. Nevertheless, the high marriage and birth rate of the civil service group means that there are quite a few civil servants who are more than a silver spoon supported by their parents' financial resources. In the first place, the reason why they take the civil service exam is because they grew up in such an environment, so when choosing a job, money is not the top priority, but children who do not have survival instincts such as the desire to belong, the desire for self-actualization, and the pride of passing the civil service exam are more prepared. (If you don't believe me, take a look at the report that examined the financial resources of the parents of the children who pass Seoul National University or KAIST.)

Therefore, the families of children who become civil servants are higher than expected. And in the remaining proportion of new 9th graders, the children of team leaders and section chiefs who served as civil servants also have a fairly high rate of becoming civil servants, so it can be said that they were relatively poorer than them. Usually, if the parents are civil servants, there is a high probability that their children will also become civil servants, and it is true that if their parents have a business, there is a high probability that they will inherit the family business.

However, many of the golden spoons in the media wanted to leave the company.

After all, people play with each other. It was the first time in the military that I felt that there are so many different people in the world, and the reason why a member of the National Assembly goes to Koshi Village and is surprised by the size of the room, or doesn't know how much the subway and bus fares are, is because I haven't experienced it myself. If a person is in a situation that he has not experienced, it is difficult for him to know unless he is a wise man.

The golden spoons that are met by the media are a little different from the people he encountered growing up. The rest of the aforementioned children, whose parents are civil servants, have a relatively difficult family than them, so it is difficult for them to continue because they have a slightly different sympathy with them. Many people know that the golden spoon plays and eats, but they have the same instincts. Even though he was born on third base, he is not much different from us. It's just that unless the dopamine receptors are more developed and more dopamine is released, it will be difficult for us to be more satisfied with our lives. The reason why chaebols, who are diamond spoons beyond gold spoons, have no choice but to dabble in drugs and gambling is because their dopamine receptors are bigger than ours. Therefore, they often kick out of jobs that lack self-identity and self-actualization.

No matter what company you're in, if you want to see the future, look at your bosses. Most of the past civil servants I met during my tenure had a net worth of about 500 million won when they retired. Of course, the environment of the parents should not be one's environment, but according to the theory of the cutlery class, it was an ironic workplace where the earthen spoons and fellow spoons left the company and the salary was high, or the class changed only when they started a business and became self-made.

Depending on what kind of environment I grew up in, my economic ideas differed more than I thought, but I know that capital income (finance, dividends, interest, rent, etc.) is much higher than earned income for those who meet the gold spoon of the media. They learn about capital gains from an early age and develop the ability to manage money. Therefore, they are interested in the economy and have developed an eye for investment, so they continue to invest even if there is a risk, while most of the children who grew up in a family of civil servants did not study economics, saying that they put earned income first, that their work is sincere, and that there is no passive income. I even think that one of the reasons why they don't study economics is that they are guaranteed a salary until retirement because this is a risk-free job.

If you are taking the civil service exam for the sake of a steady income that is guaranteed until retirement, you need to think about it because it is a salary and system that is advantageous to the golden spoons. After all, as I said earlier, many of the students preparing for the civil service are backed by their parents' wealth...Investments must also be risky in order to make more money. I'm not that kind of student, am I? If you want to pass and enter an organized society where there is no economic risk, you must continue to study to learn pipelines and economic concepts while working. It is difficult to live on the salary of a civil servant alone. The children who left the civil service were more than a silver spoon, and those who were below the same spoon did not leave. Therefore, I am going to write a separate chapter on the fact that the resignation of civil servants does not correlate much with the salary of civil servants. This is not to demean civil servants who work hard with sincerity, but in reality, the poorer the family, the more they cannot escape the bondage in this profession. I want to let you know. If your family is difficult according to the theory of the underclass, do not choose a job based solely on the need for survival, but rather find a job that is close to your potential. You need to find a job that matches your personality.

The conclusion is that most of the successful students among the examinees preparing for the civil service actually had more than a silver spoon that was supported to some extent by the family's financial resources, and there was also a golden spoon that met the needs of the media. However, those who leave MZ are overwhelmingly above the silver spoon, and the children who are below the same spoon do not leave the company. One of the reasons for this is that MZ employees can leave the company because their parents have the resources to buy them more time even if they don't earn money.

There is a very small correlation between civil service resignations and salaries.

3.2 Curiosity and Exploration

While the previous chapter talked about the painful and very realistic concept of 'cutlery class theory', this chapter will talk about the word 'potential', which can be considered unrealistic. Specifically, I'd like to talk about the complicated feelings I feel after going from being an examinee to a working professional.

As we analyzed earlier the correlation between hormones and civil service organizations, the civil service organization is more in line with the organization when the examinees are older. People in their 20s~30s have to drive on dirt roads, not solid asphalt roads. I even think it's better to go the way others don't. When you're young, you have to choose a winding path as much as possible, so that you can have a taste of the wisdom of life in that boring process. The eight-lane highway is a result-oriented road that is driven steadily ahead. It's not right when you're young because you don't know the process.

Go down what your friends call 'psychopaths'!

If you go down the path that others call you a psychopath, you think you've made a wise decision. When your body moves even a year better, you have to be bold. Although the preceding article is an article that appears a lot in self-help books, self-help books should also be interpreted subjectively according to each person's position and situation. And although he compared the civil service to a solid asphalt road, I think it would be more accurate to describe it as a concrete road that has not been cured rather than a solid asphalt.

I'm in my mid-30s now, but I think this process is the right one even now that I'm walking a different path and a winding path. This is because they are convinced that only by embarking on the path of curiosity and exploration can they get to know themselves and gradually be satisfied with their true colors. So, if you are an examinee , **you should be curious about everything in the world and experience it like a child. As soon as you enter the workplace, it is easy to**

compromise on reality rather than curiosity and live in the world from someone else's point of view rather than your own.

Based on my experience (I have worked in both large corporations and civil servants), it is easier to demonstrate this ability when working for a large company than when working for a civil servant. When you enter the civil service, you have a certain framework, and if you question that framework, you are likely to be bullied. If you're different, you're more likely to be treated as a weirdo. Since there is no such thing as individuality, you should think about "curiosity and exploration" before taking the test.

This place is afraid of change.

I am in favor of joining an organization and learning the system of interacting with others (because people live in society), but there is no need to learn in an organization that goes against human instincts and hormones at the age of 20~30, and social skills can be learned in any organization or even outside of human relationships (religion, clubs, etc.). **This means that it is less important than one's own self-identity, which is cultivated through curiosity and exploration.**

With curiosity through the eyes of a child, why? If you are a person who looks at the world with the question, I would like to discourage you from studying for the civil service. I know that it is impossible to explore out of curiosity, so the more such a person is, the more he should develop his expertise after starting a business or working at a large company. And in the boring routine of tenure, huh? I recommend you to start a business with your own intuitive items.

From a young age, we are often told to raise creative children. However, they are bound to live according to the framework created by society from the entrance examination system. The more they do so, the more they begin to limit their potential. Even if the flea **bounces out of a glass jar with a closed lid every time, if the height of the glass bottle starts to be the limit, it will not bounce to the level of the glass jar even if you take it outside. I've lived that kind of life, and it's even worse. So, when you come here, you have to have a different perspective and perspective on the world.**

If you pass the civil service, depending on what kind of boss you have, you may be able to do work that involves originality and creativity from time to time. For example, if you meet a director from Koshi, you can try a different kind of business. However, if you meet a director from the city of Vigo, you will first analyze whether there are similar cases in other cities and take the same direction as they did. Apparently, the director from Koshi, who has been relatively little involved in the civil service organization, tends to recommend items that others have not done. I have little experience in this organization, but I am in a high rank by taking the examination exam, Isn't that the tendency? Think about it carefully. In any case, when we do work that others do not do, we encounter great difficulties, fail in the midst of difficulties, and try again and again, and only in the process of repeating them, do we grow and realize our potential. **In the long run, even though better business items are bound to come out for the citizens and**

the people, the place is afraid of change. Therefore, even though each person had a different attitude and perspective on the world depending on the temperament and environment in which they were born, the moment they passed the civil service, they had to walk the same path as others. As for attitudes and perspectives on the world, according to the book The Law of Human Nature, depending on the attitude of each person, they see the stone bridge by the stream that appears on the way of the hike differently.

1. The pleasure of crossing a stone bridge (physical pleasure when jumping)

> 2. The pleasure of mentally calculating how to cross the stream effectively and quickly (mental pleasure)

> 3. Cautious people want to hike and cross it, but they are annoyed by the sight of a stone bridge by the stream.

> 4. Deciding that the hike is enough and that there is no need to cross the creek (rationalizing the fear)

Of the four attitudes toward the world, the ones that are suitable for a civil servant are close to those of 3 and 4. In this system, which is called active administration on the surface, if you claim to be number 1 or 2 due to excessive greed, you will be faced with a lot of gratitude bombs. And with the same salary and compensation, you get a taste of a socialist system in which you have to work many times more than others. **If you are currently taking the civil service exam, and you can focus on success rather than greed, and on the stability of your family, marriage, and child-rearing, then you will have succeeded in passing. However, if you have a change of heart after reading my article, change your perspective on success as follows.**

What is success?

The job is not me. In particular, Koreans identify themselves as lawyers, civil servants, professors, doctors, judges, and so on. That's why people who have a high job or are financially wealthy are called successful. **After leaving the company, I take several entrepreneurship courses, and doctors and lawyers also come to listen to the lectures. I've often asked why I'm here to listen.**

He replied that he went to medical school and law school according to his grades, but it didn't suit his aptitude and he came because he wanted to be happy. At the time of my resignation, many people in the civil service gave me envious glances as I left the company, saying that I wanted to do what I wanted to do, even though I could be paid less than this. Even though civil servants are underpaid. **The perspective of success means a lifestyle in which you are free to do what you want to do and become what you want to be.** In Korea, where there is a strong culture of comparison, it is not easy to be happy the moment you recognize that your job is you.

"Examinees. If you don't have a sense of identity and specific motivation, having a stable job will never be emotionally stable" "A high salary is never proportional to happiness."

Most of them just want to pass, so they accumulate specs for large companies and public companies, and study for civil servants. If you pass, the satisfaction lasts only two weeks. And in the future, you gradually lose the direction of your life. If you lose your purpose and direction in life, you will be hit hard as early as your early 30s, and when you have a family and are in your 40s, a job full of repetitive and unpleasant tasks tends to become your routine. Until I die, the time I spend at work is not a small amount of time. It is important to have a high sense of purpose in life and specific motivations that encompass sub-goals according to that sense of purpose. It all depends on your circumstances. I don't want you to live in the eyes of others. **Although, based only on my own experience. At that age, challenge yourself selfishly for yourself. Specific motivation starts with curiosity about the world and comes from one's own identity. If you joined the company hoping to pass, you should start preparing to leave from the moment you join the company.**

3.3 Self-Identity and Personal Style

When I told people around me that I was leaving, the most common thing I heard was, "Who's bothering you?" Why is the salary low? Is work hard? These questions dominated the list, and I couldn't answer them all, so I simply replied:

"I don't have my own color"

Then, my girlfriend and colleagues at the time

"Where are all the workers who live like that, doing what they want to do?" and "The things you want to do are the same when you get work."

Listen to the answers of the people around you

"Am I thinking too far from reality?" I thought about it for a while, but the more I walked around in my repetitive life, the more curious I became. Intuitively, I felt that if I continued to do this, I would regret it.

Depending on your inclinations and temperament, it may be a good job for you, but I decided to put an end to my 8 years of civil service life through psychological tests and evaluations, such as memories of being happy in the past, and doing things a little better than others. It wasn't until I read the book The Laws of Human Nature that I realized a little bit about why I didn't have color and why I intuitively made this decision. **As soon as our schooling ends, we are suddenly thrown into the world of work. However, there are two ways to do this.**

The first route is to start a business and start digging several wells. You are motivated to explore the world, to experiment, to have fun, and to maintain your freedom by taking control of your life.

The second route is frightened by the chaos and quickly chooses a practical and lucrative job. It would be nice if it had some relevance to my interests, but it doesn't matter.

However, along the way, both paths run into problems.

In the first case, you may try too many things and end up not developing a solid skill in one area. As a result, it's hard to learn new skills even if you want to. We have started a business motivated by freedom, but freedom becomes our burden.

In the second case, the profession you chose in your 20s makes you feel helpless in your 30s. We chose the profession for practical purposes, not to what interests us in our lives. Therefore, the workplace is now just a place to go to work, and the mind leaves work

In both cases (businessmen or office workers), they try to escape the frustration, but they feel increasingly anxious, nervous, stressed, and depressed. No wonder it's so confusing. It's a natural reaction in a time of great change and chaos. The way to solve it is to set the direction with your innate nature.

It is a sense of purpose in life.

Compasses and maps are real in life, so you have to find and discover your purpose in life. Whether you're at work or in business, at some point, you move intuitively. There comes a moment when you know what you want more. Some may have passed it by when they were young, while others may have known it as an adult and worked as a "near miss." At that time, if you associate it with your personality, you will have a new direction that fits well with your particular personality.

There will be a "calling."

We feel less anxious when we have a sense of purpose. As I realize some or all of my potential, I subconsciously realize that I am improving as a whole. Even if you don't have short-term rewards, you'll feel less tired and have the strength to run steadily. Even in wars between nations, on one side there are factions with fewer soldiers but fighting for a cause, and on the other side there are professional armies with a large number of soldiers but fighting for money. If so, even if the numbers are small, the army with a high sense of purpose with a cause will always win. Fighting for a cause means that you have the upper hand in power because you value the safety, prosperity, and destiny of your country more than your own life.

A sense of purpose plays an important role in conducting human life. They seek power for the sake of pleasure, money, attention, and power, but this is a false sense of purpose. People with a relatively high sense of purpose have been very successful, and Steve Jobs is one of them. He was acutely aware of the limitations of money and material possessions, and he was not very interested in material possessions. His only concern was to create the best original designs, and when he did, wealth automatically followed. I think the phenomenon of civil servants leaving the company is more likely to lead to dissatisfaction within the organization than it is to have similar thoughts these days. I had a stable job, but after I moved into the civil service, I lost my sense of purpose in life. So, like them, I focused on society's next mission: marrying my girlfriend.

Perhaps my next sense of purpose was a false sense of purpose to show that I had a stable family and lived a good life like everyone else? Or was he faithful to one of the human needs, the needs of the racial instinct? **I can't give an exact answer, but at least it didn't seem to be a "calling," a high sense of purpose for myself.**

check point

It is recommended that you take the test to see if you match the tendencies of the civil service.

There are no specific dreams and goals

The goal is to live a stable life while earning a salary like a gentle wave.

I don't know who I am now. / I don't know what I like and what I'm good at.

I'm content to let the day go by without a hitch.

Satisfying the lower instincts comes first.

Curiosity and exploration to advance to the current higher desires are luxuries.

Chapter 4: The Need for Institutional Reform

If one of the reasons for the low level of satisfaction of MZ civil servants is the lack of purposefulness expressed in the desire for self-actualization, **then there is the institutional problems of the overly conservative culture and the group.**

The culture of overly conservative culture is actually in an organization. With the exception of startups or foreign companies run by foreigners, it is difficult to mention the social life that all Korean workers go through. It is difficult for anyone to win people's hearts. In order to survive in it, I recommend books related to psychology, and I believe that conflicts between generations are impossible if there is no consideration and understanding of each other, because there will always be dissatisfaction even if the generation changes and the next generation comes. Still, it is true that the culture of civil servants and public companies is relatively conservative. I think there are a lot of MZs who leave the company due to sudden illness, but just as the military of my father's time and the military I experienced are so different from the military now, the organizational culture will gradually change. I decided to create a separate chapter on organizational culture, and in this chapter, I will write in depth about the institutional problems that are difficult to change without reform.

Since civil servants are guaranteed retirement age, there are two main ways to prevent their complacency and laziness.

It can be said that it is a personnel transfer and audit system. Personnel transfer is an act that proves that there is no professionalism, so it is necessary to change the system of moving departments from time to time every 1~2 years, but since it is not a group that can improve expertise immediately, I would like to explain it in the audit system and performance evaluation system that can be improved quickly in reality.

There is a need to re-understand the system of civil servants and especially the police, soldiers, firefighters, and other hierarchical groups. As I said before, they operate simply with a clear chain of command. The simpler and clearer the chain of command, the easier it is to deal with an emergency. Even if the work is inefficient, it will be carried out for the time being. Of course, large corporations do not have such a culture, but it can be seen as a more rational culture and system because employees are trained in a direction that is profitable, except for protocol specialization.

We need to specify a work evaluation system so that people who work can receive rewards. Civil servants' salaries are higher than promotions, so their remuneration increases. This means that regardless of ability, the more years you have in service, the higher your salary will be. It even means that even if you don't work, your salary will go up.

You should try to somehow apply the way you assess your problem-solving skills. Due to the nature of the organization, it is difficult for the welfare department, business department, and planning department, which look at complaints, **to evaluate the performance separately, so it is necessary to create a fair evaluation system and recognize it. It should be public, but it should give a clear incentive to each individual. Human nature is to want to be more comfortable, to be good, to be wealthy, and to have an advantage, so there is a need for personal incentives other than promotion.**

In other words, it is more difficult to evaluate work than private companies, so it is necessary to expand the minimum compensation or reform the system. If so, **there are three entities that can reward them: the head of the institution, the audit system, and the citizens.**

As a politician, there are many subjective elements involved in rewarding and punishing the head of an institution. As the saying goes, "the arm bends inward," when the mayor or mayor of a ward changes, they promote someone they know first. However, citizens and the audit system (audits conducted by higher institutions such as joint government audits and auditor audits) are likely to be excluded from subjectivity.

Rather than the purpose of "corporal punishment," it should be approached as "praise," which is the purpose of recognition of performance. In a recent KBS drama about the Goryeo Georan War, while the Goryeo soldiers are demoralized and busy fleeing due to the third invasion of the Georan led by So Bae-ap, a general recommends that the soldier Masa behead them so that they do not escape. The shocking fear may dissuage the soldiers, but this is only a temporary measure. It is unlikely that the soldiers will win the war by raising the morale of the soldiers. **In the same way, the implication that those who have no identity or color are shocked and frightened and punished only creates a temporary sense of fear rather than unifying them into a single collective system.**

In addition, the audit system is designed so that the more work you do, the more you will be audited. If you don't work, you won't be grateful, but if you work, it's natural to get dusty. The irony is that people who have done a lot of work and executed the budget are disciplined when they should be rewarded. And although this is gradually changing, the more senior you become, the more you avoid the responsibility of auditing. The executive branch of the actual work is held accountable and disciplined.

It is often heard that a newcomer like a fox deliberately makes an accident in order to go to a department that is comfortable with the bar where he will receive the same treatment and money anyway. In fact, these are things that happened during my tenure, and I want you to judge who is wiser in this kind of organizational culture. For the purpose of preventing complacency, let us apply discipline and compensation based on the capitalist system, rather than audits, discipline, and frequent appointments.

Also, create a system that gives you a minimum reward for working for your citizens. In the current system, where citizens are rewarded for active administration, only those who are in the welfare department receive them. There are only a limited number of people who say they are the official of the month and hang them in the city hall every month. In addition, the people in charge and the citizens should converge together to create a win-win system. This means that in addition to malicious complaints, praise complaints should also be heard. Isn't it because the system is set up in such a way that the people in charge are just insulted and there is not a single degree of job satisfaction and pride? It is doubtful that they will be able to afford an administration that can help the citizens. No matter how much service and responsibility are prioritized, it's time for a change.

Reform of the civil service collective system / How to diversify praise and rewards

1. Give them a variety of rewards for their personal gain. (Don't limit your extra income)

2. Think about how to redirect gratitude along with discipline. (If you do a lot of work, give them a reward.)

3. Don't guarantee retirement age. Help them develop their own identity and identity. (Let's also increase the authority of the person in charge, since the person in charge is also responsible anyway, so it doesn't make sense to do what is told from above and be disciplined yourself.)

4. Reward them with a variety of educational and educational outcomes to foster professionalism. Systematize performance rewards for work performance, not diligence. Ensure consistent work for the people and citizens, not work driven by politicians' promises. (Isn't it embarrassing, if you're in a technical position, try to improve your professionalism; when I was in a big company, they trained me in detail for at least three months in order to pamper me.)

5. Change your concept of a team so that you can rely on each other and get along with each other. Stick together as a team, not as a nominal team, so that you can run for one purpose.

4.1 Salary and Marriage of Male Civil Servant

sAfter moving into the civil service, my first salary was less than half of the starting salary I had at a construction company in the first district. In recognition of my 2 years of experience in the military (22 months with the 09 military number) and construction work, I started with a 9th grade 5.8 salary. At that time, in 2015, the annual salary of civil servants was roughly 30 million won below the salary of the 3rd salary of men, and the salary of the 1st salary of women was about 1.7 million won per month. The starting salary I received from the construction company was about 61 million won before tax (excluding bonuses), so I received less than 1/2 of my salary at the time. (Overtime pay has a lot of impact on my salary, but I've rarely worked overtime.)

I knew it and I was going to do it even if I got paid, and after I opened my first paycheck, I never opened my pay stub until I left the company. Only the direct debit text message comes from Hana Bank.

Since I was paid less and my work was relatively easy, I would have traded less pay and hours.

I worked from 6 a.m. ~ 9 p.m. while working as a contractor, so there were definitely things that could offset the shortcomings, so there were no complaints. In general, children who started their first job as a civil servant were greatly disappointed.

Let's take a closer look at the salaries of ordinary civil servants.

The salary of civil servants is divided into three installments. (1st, 10th, 20th)

Monthly salary includes basic salary (20 days) / allowance (1 day and 10 days, bonus (holiday bonus)) / performance bonus (1 time a year / March ~ May).

Allowances, except for basic salary, differ even for civil servants of the same rank. If you work at a local business office (water supply, river management office, etc.) belonging to the city, **you may have a gap of 50~1 million won or more with the organization with the lowest salary.**

Base salary

The table above shows the basic salary of ordinary civil servants in 2024. Since the COVID-19 pandemic has not been reflected as much as the inflation rate, you can sometimes see placards posted in front of city halls and government buildings asking public employee unions to raise wages. My friend's salary, which works at a large company, also increased more sharply after COVID-19, and it also happened to my girlfriend, who works at a public company. This is because public companies and large corporations have reflected salaries in line with the inflation rate.

Base salary in 2024

Allowances (full-time pay, overtime pay, family allowance, certificate (technician, industrial engineer or higher), special work allowance, emergency work, etc.)

The allowance that comes out on the 1st comes with various allowances (except for overtime pay). The full-time allowance comes out in January and July, and it is quite salty as the annual leave accumulates. The family allowance varies depending on the family member, and you can think of it as an average of about 100,000 won. The certification allowance is the allowance that technical workers receive. (30,000 won for an industrial engineer and 50,000 won for an engineer, and it is the same as 50,000 won for a technical engineer) / Since technical workers are bound to obtain articles related to their university majors, more than 90% of technical jobs are paid.

Overtime pay

Overtime pay is given for 10 hours of basic hours even if you do not work overtime, and the hourly wage varies depending on the grade, and there is a limit to overtime pay depending on the organization. Tax-free boroughs have a limit of about 30 hours a month, so you can't get paid even if you work more. On the other hand, in municipalities and municipalities where taxes are well collected, it is 50~100 hours, so even if you are only level 7 or higher, it is acceptable. There are also many people who eat dinner at the bookkeeping restaurant (free) and just sit there to make up for their overtime pay. **If you make up the overtime allowance, 100 hours x 11,602 won = 1,160,200 won, which is quite high.** In the case of emergency work, they were also paid overtime, but it seems that there will be a standard from 2024. Emergency work is often used as emergency work in snow, rain, forest fires, etc. Like on-call jobs, there is a controversy between men and women, and it is changing to a culture where both men and women must stand.

Bonus (Holiday), Performance Bonus (S~B)

Bonuses are given during the holiday bonuses of New Year's Day and Chuseok, and are calculated according to the main salary, so the higher the rank and salary, the more different it is.

In the case of a controversial performance bonus within the organization, a **one-year evaluation is given in March~May. Regardless of the salary, the amount of money you receive varies depending on your rank and grade.** The reason for the controversy is that, as I said earlier, it is difficult to evaluate the performance of civil servants, so it is not a structure that is received by those who do a lot of work. Usually, if they are of the same grade, those with more years of service will receive higher grades, and if their years of service are similar, older people will receive higher grades. Therefore, if you have just been promoted or if you are young, you will receive a lower grade.

Other allowances / Elections (poll clerks, counting clerks), on-call duty, welfare points (various affiliated places), emergency work, travel expenses, etc.

If you work as a poll clerk or counting clerk in every election, you get paid less than the minimum hourly wage. If you are a polling clerk, you go to work at 5:30 a.m. and work until 7 p.m. They give money in a fixed amount without proportion to the time. Everyone doesn't want to do it, so low-level employees are forced to do it, or they draw lots fairly. There are about 10 polling clerks assigned to each school, eight of whom are public servants and two of whom are school teachers. Teachers at school also said that they are assigned in order of time, and everyone says they don't want to do it.

On-call allowances are also highly controversial. Each institution gives a fixed on-call allowance, so it is different, but **it is about 5~70,000 won. This is also less than the minimum hourly wage, and one of the most controversial reasons is the male/female conflict.** In the past, civil servants were mostly men, so they worked about once a month on a rotational basis, but now the civil servants are overwhelmingly women. In the past, as civil servants began to retire slowly, the proportion of women increased, and male civil servants began to stand on duty 3~4 times a month for less than the minimum hourly wage. Currently, depending on the autonomous district, there are institutions where men and women are on duty, and there are institutions where only men are on duty. Everyone has to suffer from all kinds of complaints all night long because of the work they don't want to do. There are so many people who call me after drinking and complaining about life. On the other hand, the on-call staff at the outside office does not even receive a phone call It is relatively very comfortable, so if you work in a local office, everyone wants to be on call. Since the number of people is small, it is necessary to enter once a week, and **if you are on call about 4 times a month, you will receive 300,000 won in real wages, so you will earn a lot of salary here. There are many places where you stand an average of twice a week. If it is 8 x 70,000 won = 560,000 won.**

Welfare points can be used like cash. It depends on the position and the number of years of service, but **you can think of it as an average of 1 million won ~ 2 million won per year.** Since it cannot be carried over to the next year, many people buy clothes with welfare points. I bought a desktop or a MacBook, and if I go beyond the amount, I can buy it including my own expenses, so I can buy the product beyond my welfare points. Welfare points also vary depending on the organization, so some boroughs receive more than they belong to the city.

In the past, travel expenses could be received even if you did not go on a business trip. And **if you put a 4-hour business trip on it, you will have 20,000 won a day.** Now, since the citizens and the public began to know, the audit has come in very tightly, so I will never be able to get travel expenses to Gara. When I worked for 15 years, everyone was able to travel on a business trip, so I could get about 400,000 won a month. **However, when a citizen found out about the facts, he reported it to the Civil Rights Commission, and a joint government audit and an audit by the Comptroller and Auditor General began, and everyone who had been sent to Gara was spit out.** Even now, if you travel for more than 4 hours, you get 20,000 won as a flat rate, but you don't often have to travel for 4 hours out of 8 hours of work, and **since the audit came in strongly, you don't even have to go on a business trip. It can be said that in the past, government employees had quite good travel expenses.**

Proctoring Allowance

There is a divide between likes and dislikes within the organization, and they are recruited to supervise various examinations, from state-administered certifications to civil service examinations for the 5th, 7th, and 9th grades, and nursing staff exams. **This is also not set as an hourly wage received per hour, but at a fixed rate. The longer the test time, the higher the amount of pay you will receive, but it is not an hourly wage, so you will not be efficient per hour.** Therefore, the shorter the exam time and the less sensitive the examinees are (absolute assessment, certification test), the more people apply. On the other hand, like the civil service exam, the examinees are sensitive and tend to avoid the examination proctor, which has a lot of complaints, so it is done by lot or turn. You can do a number of state-sponsored proctoring exams, so if you continue to apply as a proctor, you can increase your salary.

Deduction: A lot of money is taken away from civil servants' pensions / There are a lot of complaints from the younger generation.

If you are an employee, the insurance deductible is the same. The business owner gives you 50 as a percentage, so you only have to pay 50. **However, the controversial civil service pension (contribution) is the most dissatisfied among the younger generation. With the current structure, you are not allowed to receive as much as you**

pay, so you pay more and receive less. As civil servants' pensions are depleted, the demand of the younger generation is that it should be integrated with the national pension.I remember that the Administrative Mutual Aid Association allowed you to deduct and save from your salary at an interest rate higher than the general market rate, and the upper limit was changed during the tenure period, so it was possible to save from 1 million won to 2 million won. School lunch expenses are also deducted from the salary, but there was a time when the mayor of the ward pushed the catering company to a company he knew and made a paper lunch ticket and sold it hard. Welfare varies a lot depending on the head of the institution, and employees who belong to the city are often treated more reasonably than the ward office.

Therefore, depending on the opinion of each institution and the head of the institution (ward mayor, mayor), there will be a difference in salary, such as employee welfare and restrictions on overtime pay. If you pass the civil service as your first job without any other experience, your monthly salary will be around 200 real wages. Men start with the third salary, so they get about 100,000 won more than the women, and as the salary increases, the salary gap widens, so it gets bigger and bigger.

Now let's talk about the marriage of a man and a woman in civil service, which is correlated with salary.

When I left the company, every time I was promoted to the 7th grade and 8th year, the salary went down by 1, so I know that it is about 6+5.8 roughly 11~12 salary. The salary then rises to the level of most medium-sized companies. For those who have accumulated years of service, the salary is not very small. Of course, it depends on your personal circumstances, but unless you increase your extra income through finance or pipelines, and unless your parents help you, I think it's not enough salary to raise a child as a single earner. **This means that male civil servants are less popular as marriage partners than women.**

A man is a man of ability or financial power

It is one of the instincts of women, and when it comes to becoming a civil servant, it is a matter of course for female employees or teachers of public enterprises, and even female civil servants do not care about it at first. Female civil servants are still highly aware of society. As for the marriage preferences of female civil servants, they prefer professional jobs the most, followed by major national public enterprises. Therefore, just as when you are in your 20s, you choose each other's products, and the marriage market is very competitive. Therefore, there are quite a few women who cannot compromise and give up on marriage. However, when women who have compromised with reality reach the age when they are in a hurry to get married, they end up finding a mate in it. In today's world, where it is essential to have a double income because they are in the same environment, when a woman is over 30, male civil servants gradually become an option for marriage.

'A woman's appearance or age'

Pretty female civil servants often marry professional lawyers and prosecutors, followed by male public companies and female civil servants, followed by civil service couples. Women spend more than half of their salary on their appearance and body shape.

Seniority Division / Marriage between Men and Women

It is a table in which a marriage information company divides people into grades and divides them into ranks, and even if men and women are in the same 9th grade, the difference in grades is divided. I believe that the media also plays a role in the atmosphere of not getting married, and even if marriage is an economic contract, the culture of seniority is heartbreaking. **There are quite a few of my friends who say that they gave up on marriage the moment they joined a small business.**

When men and women put their values first in the media, it means that they prioritize their values while their jobs and salaries are pre-satisfied. **The civil service is a relatively good job for women to marry, and since the current administrative job has become a society in which women are more than women, men are perceived as a job that pays less and is not treated well.** Even with such a small salary, what really surprised me while I was at the city hall or ward office was that women spent most of their salaries traveling abroad, shopping, looking good and taking care of their bodies, and men saved up anyway to become marriage partners, but their salaries were not enough. So, as I said in the theory of the bottom class, it can be a decent job for men depending on their parents' wealth, but if not, it is not a good job for marriage.

Why even well-respected female civil servants leave the company

In many ways, it is a lucrative profession for women, but the reason why they are kicking out the door is because of the development of general intelligence. **If you have a high general intelligence, you will calculate your worst moves. Imagine quitting your job and finding yourself in the worst situation and danger.** You don't starve yourself if you leave your job, and you don't go homeless and go to the station to sleep on a sheet of newspaper. You can solve your need to survive for a while by working part-time, and even a full-time part-time job pays a higher salary than a level 8 or 9 civil servant. **The fact that you are pursuing a career in a field that interests you in the long term, leaving your full-time and part-time jobs, makes the gap widen even more in your future life.**

When you experience something you're interested in, you're constantly getting feedback on what you're going to do next, so you don't know if you're fighting a different battle with growth in the first place. If we look back at the meaning, it means the will and drive to go to a bigger place with the original color (identity) through the experience of the field of interest, rather than defining the job as oneself.

What if the years of service accumulate?

Even if the salary is small, the steady income that comes in until retirement is also a strength that is recognized by businessmen and those who work for large companies. So, when the years accumulate, it is a job that even those who have created cash flow and pipelines are contemplating leaving the company. If you start from scratch with no property bequeathed to you by your parents, **the lower your tenure, the more likely you are to think that it is not an easy job unless you have a strong sense of responsibility.**

check point

Let's take a look at the salary chart of civil servants right now and tap on the future asset calculator.

Future Assets Calculator (lifetime current earnings / hours)

Example: Average annual salary of 50 million won x number of years of service (20 years)

/ 8 hours x 250 x 20 years

4.2 Organizational Culture / The MZ Generation's Rebellion

After the reserves, I became a civil defense, but I still dream of joining the military from time to time.

As someone who has been in charge of young people in the military, I had a lot of concerns about how to write about organizational culture. I also have a process from being a young corporal to becoming a madman in my own way.

It was such a loose military number that after I became a corporal, I was blessed that there were only 3~4 people above me in our company. However, because of the many bad things I had experienced when I was a corporal, the military bundlers who were similar to me at the time had told each other, "If we become Corporals, we won't do that."**And we began to get rid of our own vices one by one. However, even though the vices had decreased, the contents of the letters from the first class were quite dissatisfied. 'Well...If we don't even have half the abuses we suffered, why are the kids so dissatisfied?'** The corporals had met and held a meeting, but they could not know what was on their minds.

Through a conversation with a private on the night shift, I learned why there were so many complaints.

"Jonghoon-ah, we think we're going to make you comfortable."

"We've been subjected to so many abuses. You lie down and watch TV, you don't ask me to do laundry, you go to work with the corporal when you go to work, you eat ramen noodles after work, you eat biscuits rolled in milk, you don't call me when you go to bed, you don't beat me at night because I roll you up in a blanket."

Then he said,

"I think it's hard for us to relate to because we haven't been through that situation. It's the first time we've been deployed to the squad and what we're going through now."

The answer was unexpected, and I immediately agreed. After that, my name did not appear in the letters of the heart. Yes. It was my first time. **It was the first time they could feel what the corporals were doing with their eyes, ears, and skin.**

Apparently, the corporals who have suffered together will stick together more tightly. I didn't say anything about the other siblings' bad habits that were left behind on them, but I changed my mind about not doing anything. And the squad leader's epaulettes were also suggested to the company commander and put down. When I treated them like an older brother, some of them wondered if they were comfortable with me, and some of them relied on me. **Today's military culture is also different from our military culture. The army that adults have gone through is more like a kid when you look at the army that I went through.** In this way, culture is naturally established as the generations change. I think this is the case not only for civil servants, but also for the organizational culture of any company. Professions with clear class divisions, such as civil servants, public companies, and the military, are bound to change, even if such a tendency is high. **Bullying is a different matter...**

After retiring from the military, he became a good guy at the bottom and a madman at the top in the notorious civil engineering department, and this tendency was the same when he worked in large corporations and the civil service. In a company, there are usually the most people who are good at the top, then only at the bottom, and very few people who are good at both the top and bottom. **People who are only good at the bottom are likely to be eliminated in the company, including missing out on promotion, but I think I did.**

Depending on the atmosphere within the organization, the 'culture of bullying' may change. The sample size is so small that it's hard to tell which is the more rigid and conservative culture between large corporations and civil service organizations, but if you compare the two places I've been to, the civil service culture is more conservative. **In a large company, there were a lot of things that I thought were unreasonable. Then, the deputy brothers and the deputy manager replied, "You cute bastard ha ha," and they got along well without any major problems.** When we were in trouble, we sneaked away and went to the sauna, had dinner parties, slept in Hume Pavilion, and had fun relying on our deputies and managers. It was a romantic time in its own way...It's been 10 years since I left the company, but I still ask how I am doing.

On the other hand, there is a feeling that the atmosphere when joining the civil service was relatively heavier than that of large companies, but the character of being strong and weak has not changed. I wasn't bullied, but now that I think about it, I think some of my bosses didn't like me. In every organization, there are bound to be one or two people who don't like them...There is such an atmosphere here that it is difficult to play pranks on the boss. Of course, I was one of those people who went to work to make fun of my bosses, and I always played the role of a military captain who craved them.

In any case, there are still many young civil servants who commit suicide because they are bullied in what is called an irrational culture. When a ninth-level civil servant politely refused to his superiors in protest against the culture of "bullying" during his tenure, he and all the employees were bullied. And the young civil servant, sadly, took his own life two years ago.

There was a lot of culture of bullying in large companies, but since this article is written for examinees, let's just write about the culture of bullying in the civil service organization,

Gaps in 2015

The youngest is the first to go to work, wiping down the desk of the chief and manager, and the coffee drinker makes coffee in time for work.

When the boss is on duty, the whole team has to eat dinner together, so they are forced to work overtime.

There is a fixed shift to eat lunch with the bosses.

If you have a dinner with another organization, you will be forced to join the dinner party to save the team leader or the manager.

In the talent show held every year, new employees are forced to participate and perform a talent show such as dancing or singing.

There was a top-down culture. Also, when my boss said something, I had to pick up a notebook and pretend to write it down.

The lower the rank, the earlier the clock-in time and the later the clock-out time.

I was often forced to work overtime. There were a lot of bosses who sat still and took overtime pay, so if I said I was going to go out for dinner alone, they would notice.

The youngest was in charge of watering the orchids in the manager's care.

The boss had a better car, a watch and things like that were impossible.

You can't get on the elevator before your boss, you can't get off

Being a madman, I didn't do all of the above. My older brother, who had a higher rank, took over, but there were times when he felt bad and helped me. I could never compromise because the reason I moved to a civil service at a large company was because I wanted to give up my salary and "live in the evening." Is it supposed to be a sense of calling?

Sometimes we fought, but when we fought, it was really Jungde...Surprisingly, there were many times when I became close to my boss. I've never been forced to work overtime in eight years. I've never been bullied, but I love being alone. I think I tend to bully everyone else. It's also the cause of resignation, but when you're alone, your emotions tend to be the most stable. So when I hear someone talking behind my back, I'm like, 'Oh, yes?' I was amused. I don't know if it was because my brothers thought it was cute, but no matter how much I was scolded by my bosses, I was always on my side, whether in large corporations or in the civil service. And underneath it's a style that I'm good at, so I don't say much, and if I ask about work, I'll teach you and you're done!

2023 workplace culture at the time of leaving

It's okay for the youngest to come to work late. Sir, if you say that you are wiping the manager's desk, the cadres will be surprised and will not let you go.

(Of course, I wasn't the youngest, so if you mess around with wiping your desk, I'll tell you to wipe it down...)

You can go home even if your boss is on duty.

There is a lunch shift, but the managers always look at me a lot, so when I come in the morning, I say, "Uh, do you have an appointment for lunch today, Manager Kim?" Only if an appointment cannot be made, the presiding team will have lunch together.

There is almost no compulsory drinking party. Even if you do go once in a while, I don't recommend drinking.

Due to COVID-19, both talent shows and athletic competitions disappeared, so I don't know what happened.

There's no top-down culture, and you don't have to show up with a notebook.

Orchids are taken care of by those who have a lot of time, or they take turns watering them.

It varies from organization to organization, but if you belong to the city, Wednesday and Friday are designated as Family Love Day, and if you don't apply for a lantern at the General Affairs Department, the lights in the office will not be turned on.

He drives a better foreign car than his boss. You can get on the elevator before the mayor, but the mayor will admit it.

It used to be a huge conservative group that pointed fingers at anyone for being different, but that's changed in 10 years. Of course, even now, if you have a different idea or inclination, there is a culture that makes you feel like a dick. The reason why the culture of the civil service, public enterprises, and the military is relatively conservative is that I explained it too much earlier, so I will skip it.

The sad story of a young man and the newly elected mayor who challenged the eradication of the culture of gab changed a lot. Even when he was mayor of the ward, he was the most popular mayor among the employees, and at that time, it was rumored that the borough had a better organizational culture than the city. After becoming mayor, he is famous for changing the organizational culture like the borough. I think our city has a better culture than most institutions because of the sad story and the efforts of the head of the institution. However, I think that the younger generation has not experienced the 'gap' of the past, so it is difficult for them to sympathize with the 'gap' now. Since the conflict between generations is the main cause, we must be considerate of each other. The organizational culture is changing with the arrival of the MZ generation, so let's wait and see. When the digital generation arrives, the mindset is different, and I think it will be overwhelmingly different in the current culture. Won't MZ sigh again when he sees them?

Even though changing organizational culture is a natural social phenomenon, let's not bully people as adults. Don't do anything foolish that would cost the precious life of a young employee who is someone's son or daughter.

4.3 Insights from the Paper

I had a job that was closely related to my college major. It is said that a university is a place to learn academics, but our professors also taught us the practical skills needed in a company, and they also taught us the skills that are used for architects and contractors in relation to the subject. When I think about it now, it's not easy to teach non-academic practice, but I think the professors have tried it for the first time. They say it's hard to get a job, and they say that university is a place where you can only learn academics, so why don't we teach them practical work? I think that's what I thought.

As soon as I was in my fourth year of university, the head of the department called all the fourth-year students where they wanted to get a job. He gave me an A4 and told me to fill it out. Where do you want to work? Why do you want to go? I sat down for about 30 minutes to write it, and at 7 o'clock the professor huffed and called out to all the fourth graders.

"Hey...I didn't know why the professor was so angry, and I didn't care.

He gave a two-hour speech, but half of the fourth-graders were still preparing for the civil service exam. Of course, I was very lucky that when the HR team of a large company came to the school to look at prospective college graduates, I had the opportunity to take the exam on the recommendation of my professor. Then, in the middle of the first semester of my fourth year, I got a job. And after leaving the company, I also became a civil servant.

A technical civil servant is not a person who deals with technology.

/ These are the people who do technical administration.

When I joined a large company, I was called an employee and a driver, and I was fortunate enough to be assigned to a field in Seoul instead of being sent overseas. Originally, the company was awarded a project in Venezuela and was ordered to be dispatched, but due to the country's economic crisis, Venezuela defaulted on the contract.

Before being sent to the Seoul site, he was assigned after teaching various practical tasks for three months. After learning how to write reports, calculate structures, and use subcontracts, he was sent to the site, inspected by his brothers, and handed over the review materials related to the design changes to the Seoul Metropolitan Government, while continuing the construction. However, there were many things we didn't know even if we explained them, and it took a long time to get approval even when we handed over the review materials. As I learned while working as a civil servant, a technical job is not a person who deals with technology! I began to understand him. **"What technical officials do, administrative officials can also do," the word is unfamiliar at first, but it is a job that goes through administrative procedures, so anyone can do it even if they don't know technology.**

However, in the future, it is necessary to raise professionalism as an ordering organization. It is necessary to teach the practical work of technical officials so that they know the fakes used by contractors (such as the act of making a profit through design changes, changing materials that are different from the design documents, understanding of construction methods, and the ability to design structures to some extent).

Technical jobs in the civil service are more difficult to write reports than administrative jobs.

When science students were in college, they were surprised when they met business students who were taking liberal arts courses. They had exceptional PPT presentation skills and writing skills. In the same way, the papers of technical officials are different from those of those in the Planning and Coordination Office among administrative positions. He has the ability to write clearly. And if you look at the papers of the government, which is a higher institution than the local government, it is more visible. **Therefore, if the examinees pass and go to the civil service, the ability to write papers is very important.**

What is talked about and decided at an internal meeting is an act of seeking direction from each other, and the act of going out to the outside world or deciding on a policy is a piece of paper. **In other words, you have to talk about this or that, and then you get audited and the budget is executed. Therefore, it can be exaggerated to say that the moment you start working in the future, everything you do is on paper. I've worked** in both places, and I've found that civil servants tend to focus only on paper. The form and framework of the paper are more important than the substantive content. Substantive content is more likely to go to the approving authority and explain it in an oral briefing, and superiors tend to pay more attention to the framework and format of the report because they don't want to use their brains. Just as a good-looking rice cake is good to eat, a report that is not visible to superiors is a report that they do not want to see, no matter what the actual content is.

The way government officials and large corporations write papers is completely different!

1. If the official is a procedural-oriented report,

Large corporations write results-driven reports.

Civil servants use all the plans, processes, and results, while large corporations use the results (performance) the most important thing. The problem with large companies is that they write results-oriented reports, so in the process, they sometimes report to the manager to do this, and if the employees do not see results after messaging or unifying their opinions, the manager will say, "When did I tell you to do that?" / We: 😨

Officials leave a report on the process of the work, as it is important not only the result, but also the process. **Therefore, there is nothing to say, but the decision-making authority is free from discipline. So, even if there is a problem with the outcome, there is little**

responsibility, or there is no need to say that because they are not held accountable. Since the percentage of people who are disciplined for audits is overwhelmingly high, it is sometimes questioned why there is a person who has the authority to make decisions.

Manager asked, "How is the audit going?" / Person in charge :???

2. Civil servants have a fixed format and framework such as fonts, titles, phrases, and words, and large corporations use them freely within a certain framework.

By the 10th year of the civil service, the words used in official documents and reports have already been established in my head. I think there is a problem because it is easy for the approving authority to use and does not give diversity to the brain.

On the other hand, **what is the track record of a large corporation that is supposed to make it look pretty? And so on.**The person in charge and the team put together a large number of construction method reviews and design changes from the subcontractor, and verbally reported the safe and profitable direction to the manager, and **then said in the result report, "We have achieved results!" Through easy-to-see graphs, you can write freely within a certain framework. / It doesn't really matter if the font is fixed or the title or anything like that. It just needs to be read.**

I think there is a difference between a brain that examines various beneficial directions by running simulations countless times in the process and a brain that takes the time to look beautiful without giving variety.

3. The reports of technical workers are ambiguous.

As I said earlier, I don't know technology because I am an administration that deals with technology. The contracted contractors and designers tell me, but I don't know if they sometimes deceive me. If you really want to know, go to the 'Toya' site by yourself and ask the person in charge of the design company or the incumbent of a major company at Naver Cafe. It's not something that should be in the report anyway. This is because they lack the ability to review the report they brought with them, even though it is a review report. And the boss doesn't know either. "The construction method is like this, and the structural engineer is stable even if the structural design is changed like this," is only a rough summary of the contents, but the technical officials cannot know the details of how the structure was changed.

In the end, the budget was changed like this ~ and the construction method was changed to this for this reason, but I don't know exactly what calculation the construction method used to derive this result, but according to the review of the contractor and the designer, this is how it should be done~. Therefore, rather than the actual content of the content, it **is also better for the boss to say, "Well, the title, the font, the word like this? Like that? You'll find yourself looking pretty as you think about it. Girls won't look that pretty when they're flirting.**

After all, the civil servant is the agency that orders and supervises the business, but he becomes an artist who beautifies the reports from the big corporations rather than the content of the technology. Large corporations can easily inform their officials of the review report and prepare a report for them in order to expand the benefits of design changes. Process reports are rarely approved by superiors.

4. Get audited through paper.

Cry and laugh at a single word. Matters that will be problematic in the future may be written in a neutral manner or ambiguously. In this way, if you set the direction of the audit in front of the auditor, you can avoid it this way, and if you hold it that way, you can avoid it that way. This is a civil servant When you are full, you will naturally know what I am talking about. It's a good idea to write in such a way that you can develop your own arguments no matter what the situation is, and when you report to your boss, verbally say, "**There is a high possibility**

of problems, so we proceed like this, The report reads: Or it didn't."
I can see myself saying.

If you think about it, there are a lot of things that can be reduced in terms of time in the civil service. A ward mayor suggested that it be done in an oral report instead of a paper, but this would make it unclear who was responsible, so it would be necessary to supplement it to develop into a good idea. They cry and laugh on paper. Even in the case of civil engineering, the unit that executes the budget is so large that they cry and laugh at every word. In a word, George is a problem with the auditors.

Since the direction pursued by the organization is so different, it is recommended that the examinees choose their profession according to their own inclinations.

check point.

Which job do you align with?

You can also find out by the way the report is written.

Do you want to go with "rice cakes that look good are good to eat"

'That's a good'

Chapter 5: Self-Assessment

Many people in their 20s have little experience, so it's hard to know what they're good at and what they're interested in. Most of us had been sitting down in high school to go to high-ranking universities, so we had little time to get to know ourselves. Men have a slightly different experience depending on their position in the military, but even that is hard to know because they haven't done anything on their own.

Therefore, you should take the time to ask yourself specific questions. In the future, the most important skill in the era of Chat GPT or artificial intelligence is said to be how to change abstract doubts and ask concrete questions. The more you use this method, the more you will be able to choose your career path with a high sense of purpose.

How to ask yourself a specific question (example)

Based on my memories of being happy in the past, is there a high probability that I will be satisfied if I work in this job? (Y or N)

Do you know exactly what you're good at, and do you have synergy when you become a civil servant? (Y or N)

Are there any similarities between the tendencies of the civil servants in the book from chapter 1 onwards? (Y or N)

Are you sincere even if it's meticulous, small things, and simple repetitive systems? (Y or N)

Is he a person who can sacrifice for someone else based on a strong sense of responsibility and not for "money", which is a false sense of purpose? (Y or N)

Even if there is no big reward, can you continue to run your own race with the mind of an agency leader? (Y or N)

If you get married with a small salary, can you be satisfied with your financial power? (Y or N)

Philosophical doubts: Why do I live?, Why is life so painful?, What kind of person am I? (X)

It doesn't end with a yes or no, and it's not a question that means anything to you. It doesn't end in a yes or no, so your thoughts will keep coming back, but if you ask yourself a specific question, your thoughts will continue to be organized. It is also a way to quickly decide whether or not to study the civil service, so that you can improve your ability to move on to the next one. Even if you have a glimpse of the tendencies of the civil service group, if you don't know yourself, it doesn't mean anything, so **before you ask questions, I recommend that you write down on a piece of paper and ask questions about what you really want to do with your life, what situations made you happy, what your strengths and weaknesses are, and what kind of environment your self is realized.**

Finding happy memories (example)

Was I happier when I was free than when I was in a rut? (Y or N)

Did you get better grades when you were free to relax in college than when you were in high school? (Y or N)

So, was I happy when I studied fluid dynamics in college?

(Y or N)

If it is water resources engineering, is it consistent with the work of the water resources corporation, which is a related job? (Y or N)

Is there anything in the civil service that can deal with fluid mechanics or water resources engineering? (Y or N)

Let's dig down on the feelings that made you happy in the past and relate them to your job. Then, in the same way, ask questions about your strengths and weaknesses and write them down on paper. If you connect your strengths with the feelings you had when you were happy, you can set clear goals with the job you want, not the job that others want.

So, are there any civil servant-type people? There may be people who ask, but as a result of my travels, there are people who are civil servants. There were quite a few people who were satisfied with the civil service, and I thought that if I could be like them, I would

be able to walk around satisfied. However, there are people who can be similar, but there are people who cannot. A person who has free will and wants to keep challenging himself is not suitable for this profession. People who are similar in disposition to civil servants are characterized by people who enjoy small waves. As people who live with the emphasis on the stability of their lives rather than adventures and challenges, they do not attach much significance to the simple repetitive environment. Work is just work, not connected to one's personal life. And there were many people who were happy at home and who were content with the little things. And one of their strong characteristics was **that many of them said, "I'm happy and content that I got through today."**I couldn't ignore my family environment. **The children of civil servants were conscientious, and they kept their own routine so well that they did not waver in their work. I think the more civil servants are in the family, the more satisfied they are.**

People are divided into their innate temperament and personality that is formed according to their environment (family, friends, school, relationships, etc.), and their values and identities are bound to emerge. Therefore, they believe that temperament and personality are ultimately the self that expresses oneself. **If you are satisfied and happy to be a civil servant, you have a successful life.**

If you know yourself and are in some alignment with the tendencies of the civil service group, then you should seriously think about serialization. Science students will choose a serial as their major, and liberal arts students will take the administrative exam, but after passing, they will be promoted for each serial and the organizational culture and working environment are very different. Instead of choosing a series that is advantageous for the exam, you should think about what kind of working environment you will work in. Administrative officials (from the town hall to the ward office, the ward office, the city hall, the municipal office, and many other departments) There are many places where you can work, but technical civil servants are determined where they can work. And the more minority the series, the more the people and the environment in which they work will not change. Therefore, you should not study for a series with a low test cut.

Liberal arts students often take architectural exams that have a relatively low cut and are mainly memorized because administrative exams are highly competitive and difficult to pass. Of all the serials, the one with the highest attrition rate is the construction serial. This is because it may be better to fail than to pass a serial that doesn't suit you, then go to a psychiatric clinic and leave the company. **The reason for the high rate of construction jobs was that many people who had transferred from liberal arts students left the company en masse. Next, let's look at the correlation between college majors and civil servants.**

5.1 Meeting Middle Schoolers in Volunteer Activities

Using the volunteer portal 1365, he goes to volunteer activities once a month as a youth mentor. **The volunteer activities organized by the Korea Youth Activity Promotion Agency are called the 'Youth Self-Challenge Reward System' and play a role in helping youths develop themselves and develop their careers by becoming mentors.** The reward system is a self-growth program in which adolescents from the 1st grade of elementary school ~ the 3rd grade of junior high school choose their own areas of activity such as volunteer work, self-development, and physical fitness, and discover their hidden talents and pursue their dreams while achieving the goals they set for themselves. Children can receive rewards from bronze ~ gold medals by external organizations to evaluate their achievements according to the goals they set (challenge activities and achievement activities). Except for once a month, when I don't meet with the children in person, I communicate with them by phone or KakaoTalk.

"Hey guys, what's your dream?, is there a job you want to do when you grow up?"

"I'm a YouTuber, and the other kid wants to be a professional, a civil servant, a big business, a professional gamer, or a doctor," came the expected answer.

Then he cautiously asked one of the children who didn't answer.

"You can set your dreams and goals as you run, so you don't have to choose now, what do you usually enjoy the most?"

I thought this cute student was thinking about her future aspirations and career, but this first-year junior high school student was surprised when I told her what I had learned after 33 years.

The student replied in broken Korean:

"I think it's hard to be happy when you define your job. The reason why I support this program is because I want to know what I'm more interested in and what I'm good at." My goal is to keep looking for things I love, and one of them is to be someone who has fun for others." It was quite specific.

"That's when I'm happy. To be precise, a private education academy where both adults and children can be taught the field that interests them? My goal now is to create a foundation."

I said something to my mother, who came with the student. "My daughter will succeed" and "I doubt I can be a mentor given the depth of her thinking"....Laughing. This student went to study abroad and entered middle school in South Korea for the first time. After the activity, I went home and looked up the meaning of job and karma on the Internet. I don't know if the child knows and expresses the meaning of job and karma correctly, but the meaning of work and occupation should not be confused.

In occupation, the word "job" is an expression that refers to a job.

For people, the word "work" can be replaced by "labor." Labor is a word that can describe work, and it is close to 'karma'. The essential word for work and karma is 'karma'. It was clear that she was talking about karma. People are looking for work, but the child is looking for work. Work means self-actualization.

It's amazing how you expressed your goals in detail. Is there a difference between education in South Korea and education in the United States? You can't tell the difference in education, but even if your goals change halfway, the child has the power to run independently because he knows what he should do and think about specifically.

Differences in education for children in the U.S. and South Korea

As high school students, many of us are divided into science and liberal arts and take the SAT and choose a college major based on our grades. In the case of science majors, most of them make a living by making a living with the major they chose in college. **In other words, students who enter college according to their SAT scores live a life in which their career path is determined to some extent.** Rather than being the master of one's own life, they think that only employment can solve all their worries. As a result of focusing only on the eyes of others, **adults who grow up in this educational system begin to have confusion about their self-identity.**

Korea is a country where the college enrollment rate is overwhelmingly high even compared to developed countries. It used to be a country where people went to college as a matter of course, but now it seems that young people are changing their mindset that they should go to college as a matter of course. Of course, university is a place to learn academics, and there is a sense of separation from the actual work, but it still has a different meaning for engineering students. They learn academics and learn some skills that can be used on the job. I also chose my major based on my SAT scores, and even then, I chose the Department of Civil Engineering, which is a place where I can get a job without a specific life goal. As a civil engineering project, the Four Rivers Project was carried out, and as a result, it was relatively easier for civil engineering students to enter large construction companies or engineering than they do now. However, economic growth through job creation in a short period of time has many aftereffects. By the time I reached my fourth year of graduation, the government had ended, and the economic cycle of the Republic of Korea had reached its lowest point with a massive job shortage. Politicians tend to choose construction as the easiest way to create jobs during their term, and taking advantage of this creates a situation where temporary workers lose their jobs in the next administration. Not only is it an economy that has been created in a short period of time, but it is also a matter of employing large corporations, and even if they are employed, the employees who worked in many subcontracts under large corporations will once again become drifters.

On the other hand, what about the education of American children? Is American education really specialized in cultivating one's identity? **I asked ChatGPT.**

Educational Philosophy and Objectives: **South Korea's education system has traditionally placed an emphasis on test-based education. Admission to higher education institutions is high, and college admissions are highly competitive. However, the United States values creativity and an education that allows individuals to reach their potential. Students are encouraged to develop their interests and competencies, and they are encouraged to gain a variety of experiences both inside and outside of school.**

Teaching Methods: **The teaching method in South Korea is lecture-based, and it is common for students to study under the direction of the teacher. Usually, the role of a teacher focuses on the transfer of knowledge and preparation for exams. However, education in the United States is student-centered.** Students are encouraged to become self-directed through activities such as more discussion, project-based learning, and problem-solving.

School system: **South Korea's education system is characterized by high learning pressure and long academic schedules.** Students usually spend a lot of time a day at school or academy to focus on their studies. However, **the school system in the United States is more flexible. Students can choose from a variety of subjects and have time to devote time to activities outside of school. In addition, a variety of support services and club activities are offered within the school.**

Evaluation Methodology: **In South Korea, students are often evaluated based on their test scores. The national exam, the SAT, is important, and it determines whether a student will enter a university. However, in addition to exams, schools in the United States evaluate students in a variety of ways, including projects, presentations, and group activities. Students are often given points based on their performance within the semester.**

There were differences, but I don't know exactly how they affect children because I'm not an expert. But the student's answer was really fresh.

Correlation between one's major and the civil service line

The Department of Civil Engineering, which I majored in, is related to engineering (architect) practice, and the university professors at the time also taught not only academics but also practical skills that can be used for work in order to get a job. So, when I worked for a construction company, I applied the majors I learned at university and the things that appeared in the civil engineer exam. However, what was written during his tenure in the civil service was in a hurry to write a report for the implementation of administrative procedures within the framework of the law. I didn't need much of what I learned at university, and my main job was to follow the administrative procedures according to the law, enforcement ordinance, and enforcement regulations, rather than reviewing the technical elements of the documents brought by the contractor and engineering. Even when I was working in the construction department, I often made design changes through the review of specifications in order to efficiently execute the budget rather than the technical aspects, and since I did not use the skills I had learned in obtaining a college major and related certifications, I gradually changed my role to administrative rather than technical one.

If civil servants are used in the country in this way, there is no reason to separate technical and administrative positions. This is because anyone can carry out the administrative procedures that follow the legal review. At the very least, if you are a technician, you must have pride in being able to handle technology, and you must have a system in place that allows you to grow your expertise through continuous education, so that you can accurately supervise the construction company and the design company. The education I received from the outside while working as a civil servant was road paving training, water supply (water circulation) training, and I was trained by researchers from the Korea Expressway Corporation and the Korea Water Resources Corporation. How do you apply it in practice? I thought about it a lot. I think that there will be more and more such external training, and that we should continue to establish a system to improve professionalism by determining the results of education.

On the other hand, if liberal arts students have a knack for studying, they often take the eight professional exams or do jobs that have nothing to do with their major. The SKY Department of Economics and the Department of Business Administration both prepare for the exam or challenge the professional exam. And when liberal arts students who have passed the 7th and 9th grade exams are appointed, they do things that have nothing to do with their major.

After all, it is not easy to move to a private company by making use of your major with the experience of a civil servant, and furthermore, there is a limit to finding a job after retirement, except for government affairs or sales. Even in the workplace, you have to

constantly cultivate your own items. Then, you should try to find your own "karma." When choosing a serial, the examinees want to choose a serial that can be used as a "job" rather than a "job" that they choose as an exam cut, and they need to think about how they will advance their careers and prepare in case they do not match the disposition of the civil service after passing the exam.

5.2 MBTI for fun

T for men and F for women?

If you don't know much about yourself, you can visit your nearest psychological counseling center to find out about your strengths and weaknesses and your tendencies based on your family environment and relationships. I take a comprehensive test, which is a psychological test that includes the Wechsler Intelligence Test, about once a year out of curiosity.

To put it simply, MBTI, a theory born in the 1940s in the United States, can divide people into 16 different tendencies based on four criteria. People can't be divided into just 16 personalities, but you can identify the big ones, so it's a good idea to refer to them. In a nutshell, the MBTI is a self-report personality type test tool developed by Myers and Briggs based on the psychological typology of Swiss psychoanalyst Carl Jung. The MBTI is said to be easy and convenient to administer and is widely used in schools, workplaces, and the military in the United States.

Extroversion-Introvert (E-I) indicators that indicate the direction of mental energy, Sensory-Intuition (S-N) indicators that indicate cognitive functions including information gathering, Thought-Emotion (T-F) indicators that make rational judgments and decisions based on collected information, and Judgment-Perception (J-P) indicators that show lifestyles that are manifested by the application of cognitive functions and judgment functions in real life

Why men have more T/F women

If we were to explain why men have more T and women have more F, it's because of the repressed part of gender roles. In fact, there are many analyses that show that young boys are more emotional and empathetic than young girls. The reason for this is that parents of the opposite sex are the first different beings I encounter. A large part of a boy's personality is formed through his mother, and a girl is formed through her father. On the contrary, they experience comfort and direct identification with parents of the same sex, so they do not expend the energy necessary to adapt. Therefore, young boys are comfortable expressing emotions or traits that they have learned from their mothers, such as expressions of affection, empathy, and sensitivity. Girls are said to learn aggression, boldness, rigor, and physical prowess from their fathers. However, there comes a critical time when children are separated from their parents and need to establish their identity. As a way to form such an identity, they choose to focus on the gender roles required by society. Since they have to establish their own sexuality as demanded by society, from this point on, they may show strength or independence in order to emphasize their distinction from their mothers. Some of the things that you have, such as empathy, tenderness, and the need for human connection, are relatively suppressed and sink into the unconscious. Men tend to change from F to T at a time when their identity is demanded by the gender roles demanded by society.

Girls, on the other hand, tend to have an adventurous spirit, or if their father's strength or fighting spirit is integrated into their personality, but as they get older, they tend to change their MBTI from T to F because they feel pressured to conform to certain cultural standards and gender identity around what society demands of femininity.

In other words, a man spent more energy on his mother than on the influence of his father, the same adult at birth, but he had to be strengthened by social awareness, and women can be interpreted in the opposite way. Similarly, there are MBTI tendencies in each group.

What MBTI is suitable for civil servants?

During his tenure, the MBTI craze took off. If you're an ISTJ, ESTJ, ISFJ, or ESFJ, you're more likely to merge with the civil service community. On the other hand, if you have strong N and P tendencies, you may feel frustrated after passing.

First of all, in terms of extroverts and introverts, E's with developed social skills have an advantage. E's talk to people, empathize with them, and relieve stress, but I enjoy spending time with people, but there are a lot of people who are quick to get excited. So, even if you're with people, it's important to have some time to yourself. E, who likes to meet people and relieve stress alone in a quiet room, may have an advantage over I in social life, but I don't think that E or I have much to do with civil servants. This is because most civil servants are white-collar workers, so they are far from a job where you meet people, do sales, and build up a track record.

The difference between N and S is that of the group of civil servants and their own tendencies. N's brains are imaginative, and they usually come up with random and outlandish ideas. S's look at life realistically and focus on the mission of life (righteousness, food, and the Lord) rather than original ideas. That's why civil servants have a lot of S. You don't know what's going to happen right away, but if you're content with the fact that the day went by and you're grateful for the little things, it can be a heavenly job.

Then there are J and P.

P is those who choose flexibility over planning, and those who prioritize freedom over procedures and rules. To put it badly, it's lazy. Normally, they tend to do things in one go rather than immediately, and according to Parkinson's Law, if you work when you are pressed for time, you will be more efficient, so you seem to instinctively use this law. I don't break deadlines, but even when I'm working, I'm thinking about this direction and that direction, so I think a lot, so it takes time to put it into practice. In a good way, it's flexible, so it can be a good fit for creative work. Of course, they make good use of that flexibility to provide fresh ideas. There are many high-potential workplaces that require originality and creativity in startups. Here, too, we can see that when the company eventually grows, the tendencies of CEOs change from P to J. Laziness and creativity are one and the same... **But if you don't put it into practice, there will be no results.**

If there is one thing that is important to a public servant, it is planning. Just as everything has a deadline, administrative work has a clear deadline according to the laws established by the state. And because of the nature of acting within established rules and principles, **J's who are driven by principles are more suitable for civil servants than P's, who are more flexible. Even in their daily lives, Js create routines through planning, setting goals, and modifying them. They are the ones who are thoroughly prepared to carry it out. They follow a routine and are faithful to their work and life, so they have a strong sense of life.**

If you have a strong tendency to N and P, I think it will be difficult to integrate with any company or organization in Korea. It can be seen that the start-up rate of KAIST graduates is high, and all of my friends from KAIST are representatives of startups and used to set up consultant companies related to robotics and biotechnology. Also, I have often seen that when I get a job at a foreigner-run company or a start-up, my potential explodes. N's tend to be really thoughtful, and they tend to like a wide range of unrealistic topics, such as space, aliens, world history, the future of humans, and climate change due to environmental pollution. **Therefore, the potential of N's is quite high. It's all or nothing. There are many N's CEOs of the world's top companies, and it is safe to say that the N's have ruled the world.** The things that are made concrete of abstract ideas are the things that we commonly use, such as airplanes, smartphones, and computers. However, **if you don't have the ability to concretize your thoughts by staying in the abstract, you will become a clown and a jerk when the Wright brothers told people that people can fly, and**

you will become a "Tao" if you don't have the ability to materialize and execute them if you succeed.

I think J and S are the most important factors that match the disposition of a civil servant. There are a lot of ESTJs who are called ACEs in any organization, except in workplaces where creativity is high. There are more men than women, and I was curious, so I used to ask here and there to analyze whether MBTI and this organization had a similar impact during my tenure. Women tend to be ISFJs and ESFJs, while men tend to be ISTJs and ESTJs. **All in all, there are a lot of ISTJs. Civil servants are people who enforce the administration and the law according to procedures, so principles and rules are more important. Therefore, S and J, who have high planning and execution ability rather than flexibility, creativity, and curiosity, are advantageous.**

5.3 Between Civil Service Qualifications and Examinations

'Specs' of joining / 'Level' of entrepreneurs

When I was working for a large company, everyone around me was an employee of a large company, and when I was a civil servant, I was a civil servant, and after I started my business, my relationship changed to that of businessmen and freelancers, except for my high school friends, my close friends, and a few of my brothers who were government employees. We live together with people in society. And you learn a lot in relationships.

You can succeed on your own, but the **direction of your life will change drastically depending on the kind of people you associate yourself with, or whether you meet mentors and mentors (nobles).**

The reason why we take the SAT to get into a good university can also be interpreted as one of the human instincts, not to rank each other. **People have a desire to grow. There are a lot of great people out there, even if they don't necessarily have a high college or job, but the more you expose yourself to such an environment, the more likely you are and the more likely you are to meet people who have grown up than you.** Therefore, in order to network with them, they shout out Inseoul and study in the heat of education. And **since it is even more difficult to find a mentor in life, I often meet them through books.**

When I left my job and started my own business, I started reading books and used to fly Facebook Messenger to meet mentors and mentors. **If we use the word "spec" for a good university and a good job, society seems to call it "level."** In order to meet people of different levels, you need to have the ability to make proposals and negotiate. What I've felt in my business as an office worker is that in order to meet people at different levels, you have to raise your level or make good proposals to them so that it's a win-win situation. Sometimes, even if it wasn't a win-win situation, they would meet, which is often called a challenge section by businessmen. Those among them who have a strong tendency to give are eager to help. So, even if you are at a level where you can't stand shoulder to shoulder with them, if you appeal emotionally many times, Some people were willing to accept it.

In the same way, there are specs depending on the job. Even when you enter the workplace, the environment of the people you meet is important, so it is usually just a part for job seekers to write about what kind of academic backgrounds have entered the civil service or large companies, so please refer to it only. I also hate the culture of hierarchy, and I believe that each individual's potential and ability have nothing to do with "academic achievement." **However, I wrote the information that people with these specifications joined the company because I thought it would be helpful for the examinees.**

The specifications I accumulated when preparing for a large company were 1 overseas volunteer work, 1st semester of XX construction internship 4th year (substituted credits), GPA 4.0 out of 4.5, civil engineer, industrial safety engineer, TOEIC 890 points, TOSS 7th grade, Korean History Examination 1st grade, and Word 1st grade. **I'm also not good at studying, and after joining a major company, I was often ignored because of my academic punishment.** Many of the people who joined large companies were SKY, and many of them were from Hanyang University, which is famous for its civil engineering department. Factions were formed to conduct internal politics, and there were examples of SKY waves being divided into factions, and Hanyang University was the main force among the Inseoul faction. And then there was the Jigeguk faction, like me. **There are many cases where the SKY faction, which is at the top of the food chain, pulls each other together and is promoted to the position of manager.**

Civil servants don't need specs, they just need to take the test better than others. It is divided into two parts, an exam and an interview, but as long as you don't make any strange noises, you will pass. Divided by grades, 1.1~1.2 times revision is also required to pass the written test, and those who do not score 1 times will fail after the interview. If you are within 1 multiple of the quota, you will pass 99.99%. When science students become civil servants, more than 80 percent of them are from their host countries. If you take the test in Cheongju, you will be from Chungbuk National University, if you take the test in Daejeon, you will be from Chungnam National University, and if you take the test in Jeonju, there are many people from Jeonbuk University. In addition to the civil service, science students are among the companies that can join engineering, Since they were dispersed into construction companies, they had an advantage over liberal arts students, but it was difficult for liberal arts students to get a job, so the specifications of administrative officials were high. 30~50% of the population is from the city of Central and Apocrypha, and the rest of the proportion is from the country where they live. **Most of the other SKY graduates are from the Administrative Examination (Level 5 civil servants).**

I only know about public companies from the people in charge of the organizations I collaborated with on my work and my girlfriend's cardera. When I was in the Construction Management Headquarters, I worked with the Korea Expressway Corporation, when I was in the Construction and Sewage Team of the Ward Office, I worked with the Water Resources Corporation, and when I was in the Urban Development Division of the City Hall, I worked with LH. The people in charge I worked with were all highly educated, and judging by my girlfriend's carda, the specs of a major public company were quite high. **I remember my girlfriend whining about how hard it was because of school politics, so it seems that there is a culture of dividing into factions and trying to take care of each other.**

One of the biggest differences between large corporations and civil servants is that the civil service organization is an academic-oriented society, and it is divided into factions, except for those who are from high school **backgrounds, and there is no internal politics.** The civil servants were divided into factions and were busy taking care of each other, but the 7th and 9th level recruits were not divided into academic formations to form cliques. Rather, it was more about where the high school was from.

If you decide to become a civil servant, go like the horn of a cow!

It is said that from 2025, changes will also begin to occur in the civil service examinations of the 7th and 9th grades. NCS, which has been used in public companies and large corporations in the existing memorization-based test, will be introduced. **This has changed the conditions in favor of the candidates, and it seems that the organization of the civil service will evaluate not only their sincerity but also their problem-solving skills.** By 2024, if I was ready to become a civil servant, I wouldn't have accumulated specs. Even then, if he failed the exam, he was not favored by companies because he was old, and it was difficult to apply for a public company because he did not have specifications. **Opportunity cost was a really important test. However, since the job seekers have been unified into NCS while accumulating specs, they can apply to any organization.**

The civil service exam, which will be held until 2024, will include two major subjects: Korean language, English, Korean history, and major subjects. If you are in an administrative position, you can take two elective courses. As with all exams, the civil service exam has a lot of imaginary numbers. In other words, if the competition ratio is 100 to 1, the actual competition ratio is about 20 to 1. In 2015, when I passed, it was about 130 to 1 for national jobs, 80 to 1 for Seoul and 33 to 1 for local jobs. While I was working, I was lucky enough to pass the first round of appraisers. I studied for the second exam on self-development leave available from the 5th year, With my study head, it was difficult to pass in one year. Also, the PSAT, which is a 5th grade test that I took out of curiosity, was also quite difficult, and the second round was uhhhhI'm not going to tell you. **I think that the civil service exams for the 7th and 9th grades are much easier than the professional and 5th level exams.**

(Applicable until June 2024 local job examination)

If you look at the subjects, the basic Korean language and English are too advantageous for those who are already close to the passing line. Those who are already familiar with English, such as SAT, TOEIC, TOEFL, and TOSS, have a fairly high foundation. Even if you don't study, you get a score that is close to passing. Korean history is a subject that is easy for anyone to get a grade in. Strategic courses are subjects in which you can get higher grades than others, and it is difficult to pass if you choose Korean history as a strategy course. If you are a technical civil servant, you will have two major subjects that you learned at university. I think it is difficult for liberal arts students who do not have a college major to take the technical exam. Since science students have an advantage over liberal arts students, many people who come to engineering colleges are left to work as architects and contractors. Therefore, it is less competitive than administrative jobs.

On the other hand, liberal arts students try to study for technical jobs with low cuts and low competition rates, rather than the highly competitive administrative exams. In general, the most popular serial is the construction profession. Mechanical and civil engineering jobs are difficult for liberal arts students because they are not familiar with physics because mechanics are involved, but architecture jobs have only a small number of 3~5 problems in mechanics, and most of them are memorized subjects. It is the serial that liberal arts students challenge the most, and even if they pass, it is the serial with a high attrition rate. Then, if there is a basic base for English and Korean language among the five subjects, the time to study for the exam will be reduced, and since Korean history is a subject that anyone can easily score, it is common to choose one of the two majors for strategic subjects.

Know-how and efficient learning method / technical (civil) serial

- The base is very important for studying civil service. (Basic base: English, Korean)

- It can be difficult for those who have never studied with their buttocks.

- It's easy for people who were good at structural mechanics or applied mechanics in college.

(It's easier than the midterm and final exams I took as a major, but if you think of it as a civil engineer writing level, you won't be able to avoid it.)

- Reinforced concrete engineering has a high memorization ratio, but it is necessary to memorize it based on high comprehension to be able to solve it even when you go to the test site.

- Strategies courses are required. (Korean history is easy for anyone to become a strategic subject, so you should choose another strategic subject.)

- There is not enough time to solve English for the civil engineering civil service examination.

(There are 20 questions in applied mechanics and 15 questions in reinforced concrete engineering, and there are no scientific calculators.)

- If you have a good basic English base, you can save time, but it will be difficult to allocate time.

(A month before the exam, you should practice allocating your time a lot through practice tests.)

- The civil service examination for technical workers must be completed within one year (at least two years).

(This is because the opportunity cost of not having a spec to apply to another company is an important test.)

- The basic book is the most important. The more you read the basic book, the more you begin to see things you can't see. This is the time when it matters.

(Don't change the basic book, make a note of what you think you need while studying)

- Instructor selection is important. After all, studying is something you do on your own. However, the reason why the choice of instructor is important is that when you read the broad framework of the exam direction through a quick one-time reading, you can see the importance in the thick basic book.

- Take an online lecture if you can. Listening to lectures is definitely not studying. Class 9 exams can be self-taught, but as described above, it is one of the ways to quickly identify the style and trend of the exams.

- I believe that studying for the civil service exam requires at least 6 hours a day.

I have opened an exit counseling room in the KakaoTalk open chat room, and many people ask me how to study for the exam in reverse.They give me information about whether the basic book comes first, whether the exam questions and practice tests come first, and they keep asking for information. Chairman Powell, who sets the benchmark interest rate in the United States, is also said to use the 40/70 rule.

First. If up to 40% of the information is not entered into the brain, it will not make a decision.

Second. More than 70% of information is not entered into the brain. When you get to around 70%, you make a decision.

Too much information can be a hindrance when deciding on a direction for studying, so I recommend that you start with it.

Chapter 6: Considering Leaving the Civil Service?

With the voice actor's voice, "Goodbye, Everyone" provides catharsis for a short office worker. In addition, it is said that the world is suddenly in an era where entrepreneurship is encouraged, and various self-help books are just pouring out.

Self-help books should be interpreted subjectively according to your own situation, and like a book, eh? Oops! There are people who come out with strong intuition, but there are also people who lose the desire to survive and leave the company due to problems in relationships or wrong judgment. There is no right answer in the world, but **in my opinion, leaving the company abruptly is too risky.** Of course, because of the development of general intelligence, I know that I will not starve to death if I work part-time right now. On the contrary, if you work in a place that you want or have high potential, and it is combined with your individuality, you can grow greatly, but there are not many such people. **We don't know ourselves very well. And when they leave the company, they rarely come out with a healthy mind and body. Just as we have been preparing for joining the company for a long time, we must also prepare for leaving.** If you're old enough or don't have a lot of bullets saved up (or even without a pipeline of side income, interest, dividend income, etc.), I think it's risky to leave your job, change jobs, or start your own business. With freedom comes responsibility.

Even if you have a clear sense of purpose and motivation, **if you don't have the ability to design the environment, which is one of the preparations for leaving the company, it will be difficult to do it consistently even if you run with determination and passion.** It's hard to find people who fail in the first place and get back up and do it consistently, and **if you don't have the ability to design the**

environment, your identity to find your identity can get in the way. Therefore, if you have a high sense of purpose, you need to have the ability to design an environment that creates a routine that arises from that motivation, and secondly, **you need to train your mindset.** Right now, I'm so tired and helpless, but I'm moving my body by going to work within the company system. However, if you leave the company, you will either create a system as a business or you will have to move on your own.

A comedian named Kim Kyung-wook, who became famous for the Tanaka Award, has been steadily creating one content for seven years, even if no one is paying attention to him. Digging just one well can sometimes be a risk, and I don't know what the economic situation was, but it seems to be a de-or-ordinary person. It's impossible unless you have your own routine and a strong mindset. If you analyze successful people, you will find that some people dig a variety of wells, while others dig only one well consistently. The latter, as you know, had a high probability of success, The former had also dug several wells, but he had accumulated a lot of experience, so I think he was able to succeed. The former tend to think that luck is great. As the saying goes, luck is very important, but luck is also skill. **Depending on what kind of direction you are thinking about, you can change the size of the vessel that holds luck and have the ability to design luck.**

The reason why free will, which began with a high sense of purpose and strong motivation, cannot run steadily with only passion and will can be understood by reading brain science books. This is because the brain is lazy. When I stand, I want to sit, and when I sit, I want to lie down. Therefore, there are many people who live outside the company system and are trapped in their own world because they are unable to do it consistently. If you look at YouTube, there are people who make content about themselves as a pooping machine, depression, hikikomori, etc. Of course, they're moving again. The act of filming, editing, and uploading YouTube depends on your resilience. To some extent, you are able to run yourself. He is designing the environment by showing himself to others.

Environmental design and mindset are formed through training and repetition. It is said that if you repeat a behavior for more than 66 days, it becomes a routine, and the brain is like a muscle. Just as muscles grow through rest, even if it becomes a routine, if there is no temporary rest, the brain will get tired and give up. So, if you have the intention of quitting, you need to create a routine so that your mindset doesn't waver, take a break, and train yourself to go back to the routine. In order to steadily move toward a high sense of purpose, I think that the environment and mindset that you have no choice but to run are essential elements. This will be discussed in another chapter, but even if you have designed the environment, in order to implement it, you need to break down the goal into specific pieces, and then combine them to determine the most difficult execution. There is a zone.

I think another reason for leaving is relationships.

People are harder in social life than work. So right now, the situation is distressing and my vision is narrowed, so let's take a break. Find out exactly why you're sick, and if it's a relationship, **no matter how hard it is, let's have the courage to go to the General Affairs Department or ask the manager to change departments.**

I don't think there's a general affairs department that doesn't reflect on the next personnel season when an employee is going to die right now. **Also, I think that the best thing about being a civil servant is taking a leave of absence. See a specialist for psychological counseling at a hospital or psychological counseling center. If a specialist diagnoses that you are sick, you may be advised to take a leave of absence.** There are no disadvantages to employees after returning to work, and there are people who go to work because they are fine. If you are on leave and think, "I still have to leave," you should learn the aforementioned mindset and environmental design skills. Unless you have a really strong intuition, leaving the company is more of a skill than a brave one. And **quitting is scary. So fear and courage go hand in hand, but at least not the phrase used in this case.**

Then, just as the examinees got to know themselves and recommended that they choose a career based on their inclinations, ask yourself the same questions as in Chapter 5 Self-Assessment. While you're on leave, don't keep tormenting yourself by abandoning your body and mind, and take enough time to get to know yourself. When were you happy, what were the pros and cons, etc....

Who can leave the civil service / Who should not leave the civil service

If the above tests go well, you're already more or less ready to go. However, most people who are thinking about leaving a job don't know what they need to do in the future, when they will be happy, and what their strengths and weaknesses are. Therefore, it is difficult to perform even the above tests easily. I'm going to describe what kind of mindset and routine I created, how much additional income and pipeline I designed, how I failed after leaving the company and started my own business, and how I'm running again after failure.

Even if you're ready, you're afraid to leave your job. But if you're ready, you can say:

'Courage and fear go hand in hand.'

My motivation for leaving the company is as follows.

1. I wanted to go on a journey to find my identity.

I was a civil servant. The people who call me by my name are my family, friends, co-workers, and the occasional complainant. They just know me from the outside as a civil servant. I didn't want to know where I belonged, but I wanted to have my own identity and carve out my own life. (The direction you walk is more important than losing your sense of belonging.)

2. I wanted to create my lifestyle.

Useless meetings, inefficient systems. I didn't want to force myself to find another job to do things that would be done in 3~4 hours, and masturbate after 8 hours, saying, "Oh, I did some work today." (The autonomy to work efficiently, when you want, where you want, and with whomever you want was important.)

3. There were many people who said "no" to their surroundings.

Most office workers prefer certainty to uncertainty, so they are bound to turn negative in the battle of probabilities. This is because the responsibility is great and the direction of the audit is wrong. (I was losing my own color, I had a strong sense of opinion, and I had a lot of things I wanted to do, but I was subordinate to the approval authority of 2~3 bosses, so I had to change the environment.)

4. It was difficult to grow up.

People have a need to grow. Shouldn't we do it after work? It is difficult for a person's brain to be used for more than 4 hours in other areas, and when they get home from work, they are very tired. There should have been more time to be in the realm of the unconscious. (Personal branding. I wanted to develop my own value, I wanted to value myself in the capitalist market, and I had to find my own brand even now.)

5. My health was deteriorating a lot.

Along with the above, it's also about increasing my value so that she can find me.

At the time of leaving the company, the specific question LawQ

: Does your motivation for leaving the company have anything in common with the entrepreneurial mindset?

A: Yes (similar to a large extent)

Q: Does doing business help me?

A: Yes (I am convinced that it is a means to achieve financial freedom and that I can increase my value from the workplace.)

Q: Is being a businessman the only means of achieving financial freedom?

A: No. (There is also an investor position, but with the current capital, there is a limit to the investor position.)

Q: Would you still be a businessman?

A: Yes (The content business is fun, and we are designing such an environment.)

Q: If you could become an entrepreneur and achieve financial freedom just by being an investor, would you stop?

A: Yes (Even if the content business is fun, I will only work in the area of my hobby and change it to an investor position.)

The motivation to achieve economic freedom is clear.

I want to share so much with the people I love. That's why I think I'll be happy if I achieve financial freedom, unlike when I enjoyed two weeks of satisfaction because I lacked the motivation of a large company or a public servant (thinking only of the instinct to maintain my reputation) based on the views and evaluations of others. Ninety percent of my worries are related to money, but I want to achieve financial freedom in the realm of an entrepreneur or an investor, and still live a life of helping others. In fact, 90% of people who achieve financial freedom are said to be unhappy.

Q: So you would be a businessman?

A: Yes!

6.1 Fear and Resilience

There are two kinds of people: the desire for growth and the desire for lack.

Trying to make oneself better than it is now is a desire to grow. On the other hand, the need for deficiency is the desire to think that if you make up for what you lack, you will be happy. If the lack is an internal condition for seeking self-identity with curiosity and an attitude of exploration, then happiness can be found according to the "need for lack."**Most people, however, try to fulfill external conditions, such as money, power, and success, which are false sense of purpose.**

The moment we get a job at the company we wanted, we are happy for a while. However, the satisfaction is quickly over, and you don't feel anything else. Successful people are just like us. When I started a startup in the U.S. with a friend, we met a lot of successful people (fame, money, status) who offered us a CEO position with a prototype. When I asked them if they were happy, they replied, "If you don't train your mind, it's the same." I used to say. That's why people who change jobs because of low salaries think it's a false sense of purpose. I also changed jobs from my first job, so I thought I'd be happy if I went to another job. That's why I think the tendency to quit their first job is usually relatively high. The two workplaces have quite a few differences in disposition, but the organizational culture is similar, and the salary is low and high, so if you want to be accepted by others and change jobs in their eyes, it is because you have not trained your inner mindset.

They don't have a real sense of purpose.It can be said that those who raise their own price and move to a job with good conditions and salary negotiations in order to get to know themselves better based on their desire for growth or curiosity have a slightly higher sense of purpose than them.

We strongly believe in what we think is a false sense of purpose, so when we leave a job, **we are afraid that we will lose the money we have, that we will not live up to the expectations of others, that we will fail when we set out to succeed, and so on.**In other words, the fear of losing what you currently have. It can be seen as the fear of not being able to achieve what you thought was happiness. So, even if you are in a company, if you train your inner self (mindset), you can be happy regardless of your environment. But when you're in a company, it's hard to realize your true inner mindset. A civil servant cannot fail.

It is through failure that a person grows greatly. I keep failing, but I don't really feel the growth of experience points because it's invisible like in RPG games, but the growth of my mindset is more intuitive.

In order to have momentum, you have to go down to the bottom to gain momentum and bounce. You've often heard that those who hit rock bottom are very successful. Therefore, the retirement age, steady salary, and stability of civil servants are good environments, but it is difficult to realize resilience because it is difficult to fail. The reason why he emphasized the need to create a routine and the ability to design the environment as a condition for leaving the company is also because he doesn't know how resilient he is while at work. Resilience depends on a person's innate temperament. **When you step out of the company system, you're the first to fail, and resilience divides those who run again and those who give up.**

The thing I felt the most while starting a business was the mental training after failure. When I left the company, I created a routine and designed the environment, but it was the first time I thought I had failed since I joined the company. No, it was the first time in my life. **I began to learn and train positive thinking. Mindfulness is the beginning and training of positive thinking.** In fact, I thought I could be happy if I learned these things while I was working, but I only knew about it theoretically and didn't experience it, so it didn't come to me. And I'm very curious. It seems that the retirement age will increase to 70 years old, and I felt that if I did this job until I died and did not take on the challenge, I would regret it greatly. As a way to find my own color, I wanted to move independently outside of the company system, not from the gaze of others, and I wanted to get to know myself. That's why I chose to start a business as a way to explore the world using my curiosity. However, the frustration and anxiety that comes after two failed start-ups is much stronger than I thought. I, too, had to sit down for a moment. **And as I rebuild my routine, I'm springing up from below.**

Before leaving the company, I first went through psychological counseling to get to know myself.

It is said that self-cognitive intelligence is the most important among various intelligences such as language, logic, nature, interpersonal relationships, and understanding, which are the intelligence learned through psychological counseling. Since it has to do with self-consciousness, **you can get to know quite a lot of your strengths and weaknesses, as well as your own tendencies and temperaments that have been established according to your environment.**

In order to compensate for what the psychological research institute does not tell me, **I did a self-diagnosis as a second step.**

He went down to the past to find a moment when he was happy. I was happy when I was free. I had the best grades in college, and I was happy with everything at the time, including relationships. When I was in high school, I hated being forced to study in the middle of school and supplementary classes. However, when I let it go freely, I started to preview and review it at university. Since I was reviewing and preliminary, my grades were naturally good. As a result, during exam periods, my friends came to me and asked me to teach them how to study for the exams. During the exam period, even if I didn't study separately, I already knew more than the exam level, I was happiest when I shared my knowledge with my friends. I used to be happy when I was helping others financially or with something else. When I was free, my potential always came out, and I was happiest when I was able to give to my loved ones.

'Autonomy' and 'giving' were the conditions for my happiness.

Memories of your happiness are very necessary when you change jobs or take on new adventures such as business after leaving the company. This is because it is one of the conditions for having a specific motivation and sense of purpose. **Then, the first routine I created for environmental design was reading and writing.** Even those who have not found a happy moment can be tracked through reading and writing. People in my country don't read books very well. So, this may not make sense, but **what we have been struggling with and suffering from is a problem that people who have already lived through have experienced and thought about. I think books are treasures and wisdom.**

For those who are thinking about quitting, I recommend that you read 10 books in the field you are interested in and 10 books on psychology. Don't just read it, write it down so you can find out your sense of purpose in detail. I never learned how to write anywhere, but I wrote to give my girlfriend a gift. And naturally, when I published a book that I thought would not sell at all in a POD method and put it on the market, some people bought a book that was not enough, and I am sorry to them, but I was happy to sell my own items independently for the first time. At the time, I watched YouTube videos of Yoo Shimin and other writers, and thought to myself how to write. Then, I wrote as much as I wanted like a diary on the Naver blog, organized it, and published it on the Bukk self-publishing platform.

If you are a person who is training your mind along with taking a leave of absence instead of leaving your job, I think that reading

and writing books related to work that match the topics you are worried about, such as how to have good relationships and how to train your mind, will solve many problems. Let's wait until we see the forest, not the trees. Through counseling, self-diagnosis, and environmental design, I created a routine and wrote gave me a clear sense of purpose. Then, based on a clear sense of purpose, I tried to start a business without capital 1 time and start a business with capital 1 time for the final goal, and one failure after another. When I came back from the U.S. and was helpless, and then I started reading and writing again, and my resilience bounced back and I started thinking positively. Whether a human being is at work, Whether you're leaving your job or starting a business, you're imperfect everywhere. **So, even if you don't have to write, if you create a routine to train your inner self with exercise, meditation, etc., it will be a great help for your resilience.**

Purpose and Goal are different.

A goal is an outcome that you want to achieve in the end of a sense of purpose, and a goal is a clear path in the process of achieving a goal. Once you have a sense of purpose, you'll be able to set your next ultimate goal. Before I left the company, I got to know myself to some extent, I was able to set sub~final goals based on a sense of purpose, and I was able to run without wavering until I failed. Even now, I haven't changed my end goal. Specific goals and a sense of purpose will be discussed in the business story.

What I felt while starting a business after leaving the company / The importance of positive thinking

It all depends on your environment, inclination, and temperament, but I felt three main things while starting a business.

1. I've found that a curious person can learn more about myself through entrepreneurship (self-identity). And while I was running like crazy for 'success', which is a false sense of goal, I felt happy.

2. After my failures, I realized how resilient I was.

3. Then, little by little, you learn the importance of positive thinking and how to train your inner self.

The brain naturally returns to negative thinking. That's why psychology books compare negative thinking to ANT. Books and writing, which were one of the ways to design an environment before leaving the company, even play a role in helping people return from negative thinking to positive thinking. If you practice positive thinking consistently, you will be able to see the true value and depth of your life, and I believe that it is a prerequisite for being truly happy, no matter where you belong. **This made me think differently about failure as a great experience.**

6.2 Unexpected Outcomes

on Musk, an eccentric genius and other scientist, say that there is a high probability that the world we live in is fake.

In addition, it is said that there are VR and virtual games that are designed to make it impossible to distinguish between reality and virtuality with technology that has not yet been disseminated to the public. In addition, there is the "multiverse theory" hypothesis, which states that there is only a 1 in 1 billion chance of the planet Earth being true.

It's still just a hypothetical. However, what has been proven by various scientists as a theory is **that the brain cannot distinguish between reality and imagination. Many** books say that if we make good use of the brain, which can lead to schizophrenia if we just think about it and don't put it into action, we can actually achieve the goals we pursue.

'Autosuggestion'

Frankl's experience in the Nazi concentration camps in Germany suggests that the human mind has an inner choice, despite environmental constraints. He says that while he has experienced firsthand how severe and harsh the external environment can be—the persecution of Jews by the Nazis in the camps—internally, he is able to respond appropriately to situations with his own mind. **This, he thought, was one of the greatest freedoms a human being had.** Thus, through endless self-suggestion and inner mantras of "I'm going to survive here and get out," he claims to have survived in the camp. As the Korean saying goes, even if you go into a tiger's den, you will live as long as you keep your wits about you. It can be seen as a meaning. **In other words, what we can choose in a particular situation is our reaction, our attitude, and our mindset.**

Another example of "autosuggestion" is used a lot in self-help books.

Set an end goal and write and read down to specific sub-goals. Turn your goals back into business cards and read them before you go to bed and when you wake up in the morning. And carry your business card with you and keep it close to you. It means **that the brain cannot distinguish between reality and imagination, so if you hint at it, you can realize the goal you are pursuing without realizing it.** I find autosuggestion more relevant than the unconscious realm and the unleashing of potential that follows. Ever since I was a child, if I took medicine when I was sick, I would recover quite quickly. Within three minutes of the medicine being absorbed by the body, the body feels better, and this is probably why. I always thought, "Oh, I'm going to get better soon, I'm going to get better soon." As a result, it is assumed that the brain actually reacted that way. As soon as my mother took some medicine, it was not absorbed, but did she feel better immediately? I used to tease him, In fact, I didn't know if it was because I ate with this kind of thinking, but I was able to heal quickly because of "self-suggestion." It's just my guess, I don't know if this logic is correct, but after reading the book, I think it's relevant.

'Unleashing the Realm of the Unconscious and Its Potential'

It's mostly used in Japanese anime and web novels, so when I see this word, it reminds me of Goku, the Dragon Ball "Kakarot". Currently, he is reviled by his fans for his hair color play, but now Goku uses the extreme of his unconscious, which may be his final transformation. Without realizing it, they enter the realm of the unconscious and their bodies move first to fight the villains. In the same way, Super Saiyan, who turns into yellow-haired, has potentials that he didn't even know he had, such as 2, 3, 4, and Blue, and continues to be reborn as a warrior with more power. It is said that more than 90% of the brain is performed unconsciously.

For example, let's say you're supposed to have lunch with a friend at work. We swallow a lot of saliva before we leave the office and take the elevator to meet a friend. This is a complex process that occurs due to unconscious neural control. Can anyone tell you how many times you swallowed before you left the office and met your friend? **It is said that if you capture a part of this unconscious action and associate it with a conscious action, you will create an individual item that explodes with potential.**

It's a ritual to make an appointment for lunch with a friend and remember where to go, but it's impossible to remember how many times you swallowed or how many times you blinked while leaving the office and pressing the elevator.

Even when we try to swallow, the body goes through a process that is the realm of the unconscious, which is the following:

Saliva is produced in the mouth: When you eat, think about a certain food, or even have a dry mouth, your brain automatically activates your salivary glands. At this point, we don't consciously try to make or swallow saliva. Instead, an involuntary area of the brain regulates this process and automatically produces and swallows saliva while we eat.

Transfers saliva from the throat to the esophagus: Once saliva is produced in the mouth, it travels through the throat to the esophagus. This process happens unconsciously, without us being conscious of it.

Saliva travels to the stomach and participates in the digestive process: Saliva travels to the stomach to aid the digestive process and helps digest food. This process also happens unconsciously and we can't control it consciously.

If anyone can easily unleash their potential or catch the realm of the unconscious, everyone will be able to achieve their goals, but for me, it's less relevant than "autosuggestion." Of course, sometimes when I'm in the shower in the morning, I think 'Oops' or 'Huh?' but I haven't used it much yet, so I wonder if I can use it in extreme situations like Goku, or if I practice, I can use it. I've had an absurd thought.

The brain still leaves us a lot of messages. That's why I recommend that you take the mandatory course of "consulting with a specialist" before leaving the company.

Consult an expert / check internal factors

It is also good to consult with the general affairs department and the head of the department, but there are problems that are difficult to solve because they are not experts. Psychiatric counseling can also reveal a world that you don't know personally. Whether you're an adult with ADHD, or that your dopamine receptors are different from others, or that you have depression, I've seen people who have found laughter after returning to work through counseling or medication in their professional opinion. Therefore, let's also calculate the probability that the problem in the workplace is due to internal rather than external factors. This does not mean that you should blame yourself for all the problems that arise from organizational culture and relationships, but if you actually feel sick, It can be difficult to have a positive mindset, so don't put it off. The difficulty in getting the right mindset may be due to a simple hormonal problem. Even in the same workplace, the secretion of nodal adrenaline and serotonin varies depending on individual differences, so people who are having a hard time at work may be told that their mental strength is weak, that it depends on their mindset, or that they can break through if they work hard. That's the wrong way to do it. However, it is a pity that the workplace singles out that person as an "ugly person" or a "lazy person." **Therefore, although a psychological counseling center is good, it is very important to go to a doctor.**

I visited a psychological counseling center and went to the hospital just in case. I didn't have any problems with interpersonal relationships or maladaptation to the organizational culture, but I went to calculate the rest of the probabilities. When I went there, I found an unexpected result. There were no mental illnesses such as depression or bipolar disorder, but there were some symptoms of adult ADHD. ADHD is caused by an imbalance in neurotransmitters (dopamine, norepinephrine, etc.) in the brain that regulate attention. Changes in the structure and function of the areas of the brain that control attention span and behavior are associated with the development of ADHD, and other causes include brain injury, acquired diseases of the brain, and premature infants.

Even though he had always practiced being content with small things and being happy because he didn't feel fulfilled by repetitive tasks, his temperament and inclination wanted to venture out into the world. I also learned that he is a person who abides by laws and principles, but who wants to break them. Even though they are public servants who carry out their work in compliance with laws and principles, I found that they are more similar to freelancers or businessmen. **In addition to self-awareness, there are two main things you can gain. It is a way to improve mental stability and self-esteem, and by learning how to accept and love oneself, and by moving from the small vision of 'the me I know' to the big view of 'the me that the brain tells me', you can explore various ways such as leaving the company or taking a leave of absence, changing jobs after leaving the company, or starting a business.**

In the end, counseling from a professional is a process of getting to know oneself better, and dissatisfaction may be higher depending on the individual's temperament and inclinations rather than the stress caused by the culture and personality of the civil service organization, which is an external factor. **When I was faced with the choice between changing the environment or blending into it, I read and wrote about it, developed my own logic and solidified it, and began to overcome my fears by examining internal factors one by one through psychological counseling from experts.**

He was a retiree preparing to leave the company before leaving the company.

6.3 Creating Cash Flow

Even while working, anyone can take on the challenge of earning extra income and designing pipelines. If you're trying to start a business instead of changing jobs, there is a strong correlation between quitting and money, so I recommend that you go through the act of selling something to a potential customer at least once before leaving. Depending on each person's circumstances (gold spoons, people with a lot of money, people who focus on spiritual values rather than material values, etc.), leaving is not a necessary element of quitting, so it is considered an area of choice.

Let's make at least one extra income.

After becoming an office worker, I first encountered stocks. In large corporations and government employees, stocks can be viewed as a different concept, and employees of large companies with relatively high salaries are more interested in stocks. It is true that when a public servant takes up stocks, he is more dangerous than them because he has to tighten his belt and recover. If you don't have a lot of assets in the first place, you should try to itemize and sell the areas you are interested in rather than stocks and real estate. Due to the low execution ability, it took quite a long time to make additional income. As soon as I got a job at a major company, my older brothers challenged me to make extra income while they were doing self-development (studying a second language, getting a certificate (technician), writing, etc.). **My older brothers often used to say, "Don't trust the company too much, you should keep improving your abilities."**

How to create a known pipeline

1. There are Adpost and AdSense obtained through Naver Blog, YouTube, and T-story.

2. There is a way to earn money by registering an e-book with know-how.

3. Move stocks to dividend investments and receive monthly or quarterly dividends instead of market appreciation. / Bank Interest

4. Expand your assets and become the owner of the building and collect rent. / It is also done by the establishment of a space.

5. Do apptech.

6. Using Amazon KDP (Leveraging AI)

7. Sound sources, photos, virtual currencies (NFT / OpenSea), etc. (using AI)

The first step is the process of collecting data.It is a structure in which the person who consistently collects and publishes data such as articles and videos on Naver Blog, YouTube, and Tstory earns profits. Even if the data is not accumulated, the algorithm can be a big hit, but if the quality is poor, it will not attract traffic. If you continue to create content with your own color, you can generate revenue through sponsorships and advertisements. It's hard because most people can't do it consistently. **Also, if you decide to leave the company, you can't monetize it in a short period of time, so those who have accumulated data while working have an advantage.** And while writing through Naver Blog and Tstory, you can sell an e-book with about 30 pages (even if it's not a lot) of articles. Naver is a place where people's traffic attracts a lot, and it is good to sell it through other platforms after processing, but it is the best space where you can form a sympathetic relationship with people who match your values, and where you can add various colors to the dull colors of office workers.

Number 2 is that anyone can be a creator. When you change from the consumer's brain to the producer's brain, you may be able to manifest abilities that you didn't know about outside of the work you were working for. An easy way for workers to make extra income is to sell their knowledge and know-how. I've sold more than 10 articles on e-book sites, such as how to easily become a civil engineering official, how to build up specs when joining a large company, what to pay attention to when writing a letter for a large company, and corrections, and they are still sold occasionally on e-book sites. Kmong and Wadiz, There are sites such as Tumblebuck and Class 101 that sell their experience and knowledge, so I recommend you to try it. **If the workplace you work for is where college students want to get a job, you can mentor them with interview strategies or the know-how they have studied, and selling your knowledge and experience is one of the ways that leads to a capital-free start-up.** If you create your own color and work while working, you can experience receiving additional income.

No. 3 was U.S. stocks with growth potential and high dividend yields.

Stability was focused on the SNP 500 ETF VOO, while aggressive investing focused on single stocks, with the exception of a few long-term investments. He began to learn the concept of dividend investing with his salary and the money he earned from stocks, and after moving into the civil service, he used COVID-19 profits to increase the ratio of dividend investments. When I was studying the monthly dividend, I tried a lot by reading books and YouTube by a person called Minority Monkey. In addition to monthly or quarterly dividends, as one of the savings, it has been put into the Administrative Mutual Aid Association, which has a higher interest rate than commercial banks, for nearly seven years, and now it has been put into various general savings banks to earn some interest. Later, when I started my own academy, I opened a college as a lecturer on monthly dividend investing.

No. 4 is available for those who have accumulated assets, and it is not easy if you are a beginner. When I took a taxi or saw a building with a monthly rent/charter attached while driving, I constantly entered the app and learned the feeling by looking at the information. It was once popular as a space start-up, such as a rental studio or a space for YouTubers, but now it is difficult to enter the red ocean. But I think it's possible depending on what kind of item it is. For example, a friend who started a space business knew the demand for designers working in beauty salons and succeeded. In the salon, I find out that some experienced designers are not treated well. "You can go to work here and collect your own royalties," he said, so the famous designers flocked to the space without the salon owner noticing, and paid a certain amount of commission to their friends in order to get paid directly from the customers. Their need was autonomy. Hairdressers with well-known names are bound to find clients on their own. They are the bosses and the compulsion to go to work. He took advantage of the fact that it was too risky to start his own business and establish himself as a representative. Therefore, they are free to set their time with customers and it is in line with their desire to work.

No. 5 is also a labor force, and I've seen people who use programs to put coding values on it, but they get stuck quickly because the app developers are monitoring it all the time. I think it's labor proportional to time, and I think it's far from a capital-free start-up that leads to your own experience and color. It's a good idea to refer to the books on the market. **When the era of Web 3.0 comes, not only producers but also commenters will recognize ownership if they come up with a brilliant idea. Therefore, if you preempt a platform with great potential for development, there may come a time when you can make money.** However, it is doubtful whether Web 3.0, one of the 4th industrial revolutions, will develop. I know that the app tech that conducts surveys has a high unit price but takes a long time. I didn't do any app tech.

No. 6 posted a lot of notebooks and color books. Notebooks and color books differ a lot on the covers, so I don't have an aesthetic sense, so I made several designs and then sold them to my friends to choose from. As I raised a lot, I began to make a profit little by little. Amazon doesn't regulate e-books that run AI translators, but since a lot of e-books are uploaded every day, I thought it was right to compete with quantity rather than quality. However, with the creation of laws on AI in the future, monetization is uncertain.**Books that are translated poorly using AI are said to be causing headaches in the U.S. market. That's why I tried to sell picture books and notebooks that didn't have translations.**

Number 7 **was profitable from OpenSea, which was booming** at the time and sold several NFTs. It seems that it is possible to make a profit now, but it is necessary to transfer the coins received in virtual currency to the exchange and exchange them. It's a case of timing and benefiting. And often, they use AI to create photos and drawings and upload them to Adove. If you are selected as an iStock image, you can make a profit. However, even this is difficult to make a profit unless you provide a lot of data. Currently, there is also a music site created by AI.

Generating additional income can be experienced in advance of the capital-free start-up (the experience of running the hypothesis-test-experiment cycle) that will be described in the future. It starts with an already established platform (Kmong, Wadiz, Tumblebuck, Class 101, etc.), but later gives you an advantageous experience to configure your own system (business).

If you have capital, it is easy to start a business, you can increase the probability of success, and you can quickly build a system . **However, if you fail, you lose money, so unless you have a lot of bullets, it is difficult to continue to start a capital startup.**

Let's take a look at capital-free start-ups.

Formula = Formula + Sell in advance / Implementation technology, Execution (One month is enough for a cycle)

It is important to repeat hypothesis - test - execution rather than items.

For those who are new to starting a business, what is an item? What kind of items are you going to sell for? Items are very important, but no matter how innovative an item is, it doesn't mean anything if it doesn't sell to consumers.

How to increase the probability of success (success = number of cycles x probability of success)

If you don't have an entrepreneur around, you won't know anything about starting a business. Beginners can also become teachers to beginners. Often, even if you are only in the top 20%, you can really make money with your talent and knowledge. With the development of platforms, anyone can now become a producer, so it's not wrong. Taking advantage of the fact that there is no private education related to entrepreneurship in the market, the person who founded Life Hacking School, a start-up academy for adults (CEO Kim Sung-sung), is also a case of setting up a cram school in the sense that beginners teach beginners, even though he is not a great entrepreneur himself. Similarly, I didn't have a place or concept to learn how to start a business, so I took a course here and learned the basic concepts.

Workers have never done the hypothesis-experiment-test cycle, so the probability of success is low. Therefore, the frequency should be increased. Just as people who keep exposing their posts are more likely to be noticed and succeed, sales should also have a basic qualitative aspect, but you should cultivate a lot of experience in exposing people.

Business, love, and writing are all in the same vein. EQ, which is the ability to form a bond between people, is not only necessary for social skills at work, but also for starting a business. And many jobs may disappear with the development of AI, but the ability to empathize with each other is difficult for AI to learn. Business is successful when you know the customer's heart, love succeeds when you know the lover's heart, and writing succeeds when you know the reader's heart. **(Business, Romance, Writing = Clients, Lovers, Readers)**

It was the ability I lacked the most, and I used to play to my strengths rather than reinforce my shortcomings. In business, you do all the systems that you used to do in the company, such as planning, marketing, people management, and taxes. What I'm not good at is also a way to put others (business partners) first. **Among them, marketing is more important to know people's psychology and understand their needs than the quality of the product (item).** In marketing, funnel theory refers to the number of buyers (consumers) from the landing page to the purchase button. Just as the funnel narrows from the entrance to the exit.

Marketing funnel (funnel shape):

The last one is 'Imitate the item' Original and creative items are difficult to eat into the consumer market. We recommend that you start by choosing an example that you can emulate. The fast-follow method of quickly benchmarking existing items and following them is appropriate. Those who start ahead often put up barriers for the fast followers who are following, so even if it's hard to get ahead of them in the competition, it's a way to gain some share of the market. **This is because there is no 100% monopoly rate in the market. However, even if it is a benchmark, a differentiation strategy is clearly needed.**

Examples of capital-free start-ups

Toss CEO Lee Seung-geon is there. He was separated from his highly educated group after eight failed start-ups. And I was left alone, and I was like, 'Ha...It will fail this time as well, right? Let's try it one last time," he created a financial settlement system called Holo Toss. At first, there was no system, just a hypothesis and experiment, and in order to keep the promise made to customers, he paid a direct fee and transferred it to his account. At that time, free fees and fast remittances were groundbreaking. Lean startups are like hypothesis-verification-execution. In the verification stage, it is a process of knowing the needs according to how much traffic is attracted, so it is often determined at this stage. Even if you put your heart and soul into a novel idea and make a good product, it is meaningless if there are no consumers, so most successful entrepreneurs start very lean when they continue with the verification stage and execution. Do an experiment With the system in place as much as possible, CEO Lee Seung-geon at the time **immediately experimented with a landing page that he made roughly with a Facebook ad that said, "A service that makes remittances easy and can be settled in 10 seconds."** And when we got a lot of traffic in one day, I thought, 'Is this going to work?' While doing so, we continued to develop while receiving feedback from customers.

[Definitions]

Lean Startup: It is a method of quickly bringing products and services to market, obtaining evaluations, and then reflecting this feedback again to promote improvements. Lean startup is a concept that was born through the combination of 'Lean', which means efficient business operation, and startups

There are also many foreign companies that have succeeded by starting a business without capital. Here are three examples:

[Case]

Airbnb

It's an online accommodation booking service, and Airbnb's founders believe that providing beautiful photos of their listings will increase bookings. They quickly experimented with this idea and achieved valid results with minimal effort. When they saw good results in their experiments, they implemented the elements and expanded the service to all customers.

Uber

Founded in 2009, the American ride-sharing company now operates in more than 900 cities around the world. Launched 5 units in San Francisco as a pilot and based on the problems and feedback obtained from this

Spotify

Founded in Sweden in 2006, the music streaming service now operates in more than 70 countries around the world. Spotify's vision is to provide people with the right music at the right time, while incentivizing artists by paying them based on the number of shares their music receives.

They also built prototypes inexpensively in the early days and released them only when quality standards were met. Based on user feedback, we set up a revision roadmap. If you develop the ability to sell your own products in advance while working, you will have a sense of how to sell them to customers in the capitalist market after you leave the company. Highly successful people didn't chase money, but itemized what they wanted to do based on their identity. In the pursuit of a high sense of purpose, a false sense of purpose often follows on its own. **But if you quit the drug of paycheck after leaving the company, I think the pipeline to a livelihood is a real problem for some.**

check point

(Sense of Purpose and Economic Reality in Life)

Imagine your life after leaving the company and write about it.

Be specific about how you're going to build your pipeline.

To summarize my exit plan at the time of leaving the company,

○ Cash flow immediately after leaving the company (cash flow) / (Monthly average: net income of 2 million won)

200 million in cash (average interest on deposits at savings banks, 4%) - Excluding financial income tax: Net income of 7 million won (year)

Dividend 250,000 (QYLD, JEPI 11%) - Monthly dividend excluding income tax:

Net income 23.25 million won (year) Cash 50 million won (investment position) - No leverage, only coin swing trading

60,000,000 won in cash (business position) - Lump-sum pension payment (including administrative mutual aid association) Start-up cost after hypothesis verification

○ Make sure to make a routine

(Reset your goals every day to make your life more repetitive, not just repetitive)

○ Investor Position

Coin swing, single hit (chart trading), catch real estate quick sale

○ Entrepreneur position (content-related platform business, rental)

Content-related (YouTube, blogs, books): financial and economic concepts, talking about public officials, meeting rich people (Daejeon, Sejong gathering), creating a sense of belonging, getting a psychological certificate (marketing, understanding consumer psychology),

Chapter 7: Failure

People wear masks in reverse. At work, there are sometimes people around me who are good to others and when they come home, they verbally abuse and assault their families. A number of socially unacceptable personality traits have clearly suppressed them. We've tried to be terribly kind and pleasant, but everyone has a shadow. And the more you can't face yourself, the thicker and deeper the shadow becomes.

The reason why criminals are often shown in the news and the media is that we can pretend to be saints, or we can tell criminals that villains should be eliminated from society, or that we despise them to our heart's content. Because of their thirst for the expression of darkness, they all have to pretend to be angels, and the tension that comes from having to pretend to be so right is relieved to some extent. It's about identifying and acknowledging the dark side of your personality. People who have identified this dark side with a conscious check are said to have the ability to identify their flaws and mistakes and laugh them off.

This dark shadow must descend endlessly to acknowledge and move on, and one must constantly train one's reason, not one's emotions. Human beings need to point out their mistakes and face them as they are in order to strengthen their reason. And according to the shadow that is formed, one's temperament and tendencies are divided, **and as in the book "The Paradox of Intelligence", among them, highly intelligent (smart people) often fail in life. For example, if we compare it to a business,**

Why Smart People Fail in Business

(The smarter a person is, the harder it is to do it.)

Among the high-spec (SKY, KAIST, and overseas universities) startup founders, there are only a few who have succeeded, such as Naver, Kakao, and Baedal Minjok. **'This work is logically impossible!**

(Fallacy of confirmation bias)' and making the logic of the hypothesis too specific, so it is likely that they have come to the conclusion that 'this was a difficult undertaking'. Because high-spec people are smart, they can **trace back and logically find reasons why they can't.** On the other hand, they **say, 'This is unconditional! Let's make it right (the fallacy of conviction bias)' and** have a strong conviction of believing in oneself. Spend at least 6 months to 1 year developing a hypothesis. 1 year to make an app, 6 months to build a website, 1~2 years to make a product...When the actual work comes out, it is sold to consumers. It takes three years (time) to conduct an experiment, and it costs a lot of money. If consumers don't buy it, the business will be ruined. Because they are smart, they are only interested in their own ideas. Mr. Toth also explains the reason for the failure of the 8 businesses with the high-spec people as above.

Starting a business is not a making, it is an experiment. The aforementioned hypothesis (Challenge Section: Maybe it's time to do a more ignorant and honest repetitive experiment) is often not carried out by just saying, "I don't think it will work in my head, will it work?" Rather, this is the stage that must be verified and implemented. The challenge section should be done ignorantly, and you should meet at least 20 or 30 customers during the verification phase. A hypothesis (idea) is just a hypothesis. (It accounts for 5% of start-ups.)

On the contrary, Elon Musk is famous for turning the previous two errors into concrete plans. He often uses the fallacies to continue the unrealistic in a way that is ignorant and straightforward, and Musk tells us to "Mars Gazua!" Cry out. People (investors, the upper class, etc.) are ecstatic, and a spacecraft is launched from Space X. Even if they fail, they put unrealistic things into practice, so people invest again. If you fail, people take it for granted, saying, "It's not easy!" because it's uncharted territory, and they think it's amazing, saying, "How do you think that and put it into practice?" If successful, it will be an achievement worthy of world history and humanity, and it will bring you ridiculous wealth. Musk only plays the winning game.

But unlike Musk, we tried to catch two rabbits from the beginning. The experiment was carried out by changing the unrealistic to concrete, but it was not a groundbreaking material that would attract people's attention, and it lacked the ability to materialize a groundbreaking idea. And it struggled quite a bit with the laws that had not yet been settled.

Business story after leaving the company (start-up / capital start-up)

While starting a business with no capital, he told his business partners that he had to go to the United States, and he apologized. I thought that the business of the Academy of Economics, which is a start-up without capital, would take its place, and I was more interested in startups in the United States. So I set the least stake and at the beginning of the second trainee period, I left to start a business that I had proposed to a high school friend who was the head of development at Apple. It was a hypothesis that I constantly discussed with my friends during my tenure, and it was a project that I really wanted to experiment with, so the prototype was completed to some extent. The prototype is a startup that combines green + blockchain technology in Silicon Valley, U.S., where carbon credits are managed in connection with cryptocurrency, and he was able to implement the technology while he was in the development team at Apple. Since I was at a low level, I was grateful to my friend who responded because it was a business that had to be proposed. And he needed a lot of money to meet the company's capital and the amount of money he had promised to invest and create jobs in the terms of his business visa. The investment was valid for two years, with conditions such as a certain period of time and a certain number of jobs created, after which the funds had to be spent to prove that the investment was maintained and jobs were being created in order to convert the conditional permanent residency permanently.

The three of us, including my friend who had just left Apple and one of his acquaintances, had implemented some technical skills and went to meet with some big names to offer them a CEO position. One of them, a Jewish-American, accepted our offer, and at first, his connections led to a contract that was signed without advertising or marketing.

The business we have been working on is similar to the vision of a company called 'Eco Eye', which recently went public in Korea. However, they differ only in that the 4th industrial revolution, blockchain technology, has been introduced. It didn't take long for the deal to be struck and break even. However, the business that led to the credibility of the CEO began to suffer setbacks due to technology and legal regulations. And since the U.S. market is based on market capitalism more than in Korea, they don't wait when problems arise. I expected it to be different in the United States, but the academic and racial discrimination I encountered while working in business was worse than I expected, and the technical challenges were one of the biggest obstacles in the process of doing business. The platform, which traded carbon credits with companies that continued development after the prototype, was not easy to continue to develop due to legal regulations.

First, the development of smart contracts was much more complex than expected. Unexpected problems arose during the code writing and debugging process, and it took a lot of time and effort to solve them. In addition, there is the problem of scalability of the blockchain network. As the volume of transactions increased, the performance of the network deteriorated, and a new technical solution was needed to solve it. In addition, security issues were a major obstacle. Because carbon credit transactions deal with sensitive information, a cautious response to security concerns was required. However, it was not easy to keep the system secure, and when some of the contracts were canceled due to technical and legal issues, we went back to them several times to renew the contract, but it was difficult to change their minds.

It wasn't easy to win new customers through marketing. Implementing blockchain technology related to carbon credit seemed like a revolutionary, but we challenged ourselves at the beginning of the Fourth Industrial Revolution. And as errors and security issues in smart contracts began to deteriorate the reliability and stability of transactions. Issues with the protection of personal information in accordance with the law have made it more difficult for the business to operate. Funding problems also followed. Early investors did not expect the expected results, and the influx of new investors was blocked.

The bottom line is, we didn't consider legal regulation as much as we thought. Since there were no clear guidelines on the legal aspects of transactions using blockchain technology, we worked closely with legal experts, but the transparency of transactions enabled by blockchain technology was held back. It failed to take into account the potential for personal information exposure in carbon credit transactions, and it was quite expensive to compensate for with technology. It was too risky to inject more capital and proceed, so we decided to sell. The reason for our failure was a very risky business that started by incorporating blockchain technology into the climate-related green market, which is difficult to do properly. Like all startups, we had the fallacy of confidence bias. There are so many episodes that I can't put them all in writing, but I've been in Korea for about two months now after failing in business.

We also started the stage of verification in the process of hypothesis-verification-execution only with the confidence of the representative's credibility and technology, and it can be seen as a case where we started with various investments and equity capital rather than starting leanly. During the verification phase, we were quite arrogant, and we thought we would succeed because there were a lot of companies that were contracted in the early stages. And when I returned to Korea, the business of the Academy of Economics, which I thought was a well-established business, was also falling apart ... **The time has come for me to go deep inside and face the shadow again. The dark side of my personality is stubbornness and obsession, and it reflected my opinion that I should push through to the end, so I proceeded without going through the verification stage enough. I was so absorbed in the ideas I proposed that I failed to see my flaws and mistakes properly.**

7.1 Continuing the Business Narrative

The business that continued with hypothesis-verification-execution is rather related to the capital-free start-up economic academy project. After I left the company, all the people I knew were office workers, so I wanted to meet people who were doing business. After I decided to leave my job, I went to a meeting of businessmen on a small group app. It was a group of businessmen in their 30s who were interested in investing (stocks, real estate, macroeconomics, sports, reading, English, speaking as a second language). And when I entered the KakaoTalk O-Talk room, I saw that each leader (the top 20% of knowledge) held a separate somoim to teach the members. **The leaders gathered a total of seven members to teach, and it was similar to a kind of offline Class 101 platform where they built their own portfolios every week. There** were close to 130 members, so I went to the meeting and suggested to the president that we develop the current system into an academy project. Normally, the strategy is to grow into a content business and secure personnel and then go to the platform business, or use capital to make one side a highly specialized group and bring in personnel.

My ultimate goal was to be a fast follower of 'Moonbu'. I thought it was suitable for starting offline and doing an online lecture platform business. The most difficult business can be seen as a platform business, and the reasons for this are as follows.

You have to secure either side A or side B. And we tried to develop it into a platform that can go back and forth between the A or B side boundaries. It consisted of a back-and-forth class where everyone became a teacher (the top 20% of knowledge) and a student. In terms of brunch, A (readers) and B (writers) must be composed to attract inflow. Therefore, in order to form A (group members) and B (teachers), we adopted B side as some of the leaders as internal instructors, and met and recruited professional instructors. Since Side

A was clearly secured, there was an opportunity to contact Side B, but the problem was money. Since each member of the group paid 10,000 won per month to enjoy all the content, our revenue was 1.3 million won per month, which was not enough to bring in external instructors. Since it is a capital-free start-up, when it is implemented through verification, the business license and taxes need to be paid later, but when it comes to bringing in external instructors, I have experienced the challenge section myself.

This class consisted of a 5-week package, and in the 4.5th week, we divided the real estate (auction, lease) part, and in the case of the auction part, I contacted the appraisers, but the unit price was not right, so I finally went to a lawyer in the field of real estate and auctions. In the third week, the external instructor was a well-known person who came down from Seoul, so he paid quite a high amount, so I didn't have enough money to pay the lawyer. However, when I appealed to him with emotion, I was able to bring him at a low price that did not even cost the unit price for the consultation time. The lawyer said that the young people are doing it, but I have to help them, and I would like to thank him again for taking time out of his schedule twice a week.

We wanted to launch an academy business that would cultivate economic ideas rather than fraudulent courses that bordered on trading, but in the process of validating the five-week package, we realized that people's needs were different. First of all, the briefing session was held, and most of the people who attended were people from the group, but through marketing (carrot market, flyer, mom café advertisement), about 5~10 outsiders also came to the briefing session.

The portfolio of the briefing at that time is as follows.

□ start

1. Copyfighting Draft Finalized by May 26 (Show Leaders)

2. Curriculum, Lecture Schedule, Course Objectives → Get from each leader = Most important / Training materials and samples = Create a ppt draft / Until May 26 (Show leaders)

3. Leader → Teacher (choose 1) Contact: Last week of May

condition

(1) Concept of business owner and employee (generous profit share = Instructor: Founder)

For those who originally wanted to start a business, they took classes in the class and
Make money.

(2) Co-founding concept (up to five people!) -—

As for the distribution of income, there are more teachers allocated, and if the business expands, the co-founder will be a little more profitable.

4. Marketing (starting June 1)
Carrot Market, Mom Cafe (local advertisement), Facebook, Instagram advertisement,

Asking them to advertise on YouTube, blogs, personal channels, asking other group presidents, discussing -—where to distribute flyers

5. Deposit (10,000 won) system introduced (from June 1st)
– Refund upon attendance (customer DB must be secured)
Call 3 days in advance!, text the day in advance! = Customer DB

Study 130 people How to use it! (If you want to take the class, you can attend)-—Prize (130 people in the seminar will have to ask for a seat filled without a refund system)

6. On the day of the briefing session

(1) Before the presentation: prepare paper and pencil, secure a parking lot, secure a guide, install a placard/ask the person to calculate the future asset calculator by themselves, announce the pension holding, decide on the salary of 'earning' rather than 'receiving' the importance of the subconscious mind (encourage them to write their goals on paper), motivation three: play a YouTube video (must be edited)

(2) Presentation of PPT of the briefing session / Transcript creation (before, during, and after the presentation)—Moderator

→ first of all, classes will be held in the study room, and in the meantime, the academy will be taken over and redecorated.

(6) It 's not too late to apply for a free 5-day course.

"I'm confident!"—-Moderator

Free study participation (upon completion of the 5th week) = 130 study students emphasized!

(7) "If you register now, you will get a 10% discount on the one-month fee and a 10% discount on companion registration"—-Moderator

Things to look for (before or after demand?) -—Discussion

Maybe you can look for it after it happens / Young people, women entrepreneurs -—You can look for this with a business license

However, when the management team monetizes, such as Mom Cafe, there are bound to be churners. Even though there were defectors, I thought it was not a problem because there were more people who gathered in the O-Talk room due to various marketing. And the stone bridge theory, which induces people who were induced by the five-week package to the majority, has also succeeded in its own way. However, it was not as popular as it should have been, as everyone wants to make a quick buck. That's when I realized why people still get scammed about trading and real estate. Even though you have to learn the economic concept to invest on your own terms, people tend to believe what others say and invest. According to your assets Or, judging according to the macroeconomic trends, you need to invest to not be shaken, but you often learn trading as it is. I found out why there are no academies in Korea that teach economic concepts. Of course, knowing the macroeconomy, economic cycles, and trends does not mean that you are good at investing. If that were the case, all economists would be rich. However, if you develop your own eye for investing, you won't panic even if you lose money. So, rather than five-week packages, the trading sessions, monthly dividend classes, and real estate leases were more popular, and we were becoming more and more of a business that taught us economic ideas. What you feel while doing business can only take advantage of people's psychology, so you have no choice but to choose content that is in high demand in order to generate revenue. This is where disagreements began to arise between the business partners. It started as a cram school that taught economic concepts, which are a high sense of purpose, so they began to fight separately into two and one person. Two people who want to run a long-term race and one who wants to make a profit...And at the beginning of the second term, I would often be informed by my two partners about how the business was going in the United States. When the third and fourth phases progressed and I came back to Korea, one of my partners had already left, and I failed in the process of going from offline to online. And I tried to continue again, but the meeting leader persuaded me that I wanted to stop. And since the two of my partners are already entrepreneurs, the business started by relying on the plans and prototypes I brought. It seems that there was no progress during the period when I was in the United States. The fact that they were more concerned with each other's own businesses was also a big cause of the fight.

The partners fought among themselves and sought direction, but their differences in opinion were stark and they could not make concessions. The academy project came to an end when the words "let's stop" came to an end, and now each leader is working as before. Since it was a capital-free start-up, it was an academy business that had a lot of experience through hypothesis-verification-execution. Since it is not a capital start-up, I think I have a little feel for starting a business by thinking a lot about marketing, copyfighting, and bait strategies according to the stone bridge theory. I may have started with great enthusiasm, but I was happy and joyful like a madman while running. When I woke up in the morning, I was surprised to see myself running to the business in a business-mad manner. It was exciting to be able to present my own items in the capitalist market with a sense of purpose, rather than as an office worker who rode the subway like a zombie. However, the U.S. business was still far from clear, and by the end of both projects, I was on the sidelines.

Now, in order to get back on the road to resilience, she signed up to be a writer at brunch and is writing. If you look at brunch, there are so many people who are good at writing sensitive essays. So I thought I was going to be a writer, but I don't know if they accepted question 2 and 3 because they wrote them differently than others, but at that time I declared that I was going to write an informational article related to the civil service. Apparently, a highly literary and emotional essay is too difficult for me...

question

□ What kind of writing are you going to write?

answer

□ said, "I'm going to write an informative article that I'm good at."

I've spent too much capital, and for the time being, I'm going to expand my pipeline and apply to KAIST Graduate School of Future

Strategy. Rather than capital-based start-ups, we are trying to turn the hypothesis-verification-execution cycle to capital-free start-ups, and we are going out to volunteer activities for youth. The biggest goal is to create animal-related welfare projects (such as legislation similar to those in developed countries, animal shelters, etc.) and social enterprises that solve problems such as hikikomori and youth loneliness. I think I've hit rock bottom now, but is there a better bottom? After lying helpless on the bed for weeks, I was able to run again through books and writing.

7.2 The Most Challenging Aspect of Execution

I always ignored self-help books. A bit of a low-level article? Rather than looking for a reason why they were successful, I thought, "They must have succeeded because they're different from normal people, and they have nothing to do with me." Everyone has a different perspective on success, but after reading their books, **I learned what we commonly call successful people have in common.** Self-help books offer a lot of methods, starting with how to set an end goal, breaking it down to sub-goals, how to design an environment, the importance of mentors, why it's hard for us to implement them, the realm of the unconscious, potential, autosuggestion, and much more. It also provides rational evidence such as why people end their lives without realizing their potential, how lazy the human brain is, and how it has continued its habits from the brains of the past to the present age.

"If you act like this in the future, the world will look different, and you can do it!" It also gives you confidence.

On the one hand, the disadvantage that I have felt after reading so many self-help books is that the repertoire is similar. There were only people who had been addicted to drugs or had failed badly, and it was hard to find a middle-class or higher family in the first place. And when it comes to examples, Steve Jobs and Warren Buffett are the main ones.

1. Aim for dramatic effects. (The story of Cinderella, who raised her life from a mess to the best....)

2. There are many works that create a win-win structure with famous promoters.

3. All self-help books imitate each other.

4. Books also bring revenue from sales, so they use people's psychology as part of their marketing tools.

5. Self-help books are subject to different interpretations depending on each individual's environment.

There are some books that are not intended for profit, but most of the books that show the purpose of profit or do not disclose how the proceeds are spent are imitations of Western self-help books. The same goes for business, in the first place, the fast-follow strategy is the easiest strategy that works for the masses. Unless China is an idiot, there is a reason why it clumsily and quickly copied the culture and technology of advanced countries and then put them on the market.

At first, I was more likely to read than what I was interested in.**But I don't think the right way to approach self-help books is the right way to do it. You** have to read in an area that interests you and develop your thoughts in order to develop originality and creativity, but when you read something that you are not interested in, you end up with "Oh, yes." Therefore, it is important to interpret it differently depending on the situation of each person, and it is necessary to read self-help books in the field of interest or books that stimulate curiosity to change the depth of thinking. I think it's right to choose a book from your own point of view, not a book that others say is good. Also, **following their books won't change your life. It's just a tool, and you have to decide how you want to use it.**

Nevertheless, we should meet them in books. Unless you pay a lot of money, it's hard to meet successful people.

If we analyze the successful people we talk about in self-help books,

I was mesmerized in the realm of the unconscious, and in my dreams, Aha! There is some causal relationship between creativity and genetics and childhood, but there are certain laws rather than the realm of talent. First, they **started with a specific goal of who they were going to be or how they were going to use this hypothesis before they created the item.**

It's also important to know a lot about the item you're going to do. This is because the hypothesis (item) is familiar to many people, but it is necessary to add something a little different. It is said that creativity is manifested in the right brain. Aha! Some of the things that came to mind while doing it were influenced by genetics, but they knew more than others because they thought about it many times in their brains, even if it was unconscious. Also, when I was a child, I was often crazy about one thing. At the stage of concretizing a hypothesis and executing it, such as, "If you want to be a writer, read a lot of books," you need to know more than others to be original.

It is said that people are open to familiar things. When you see an advertisement that you are often exposed to while walking on the street, it is said that it creates a sense of familiarity in the brain and reduces rejection. However, if it's too familiar, it quickly gets bored and loses interest, so you need to make it a little different. YouTube and Facebook, for example, initially deliberately suppressed a lot of features to make people feel familiar. Then, when people get tired of it (cliché), they try to maintain their preference by adding something a little different at the right time, like YouTube shorts. It is said that foreigners use Reddit a lot. Even when a meme is trending on Reddit, it is said that you have to add something a little different to the existing meme to make it popular. "The Youngest Son of a Chaebol Family" has become popular, and web novels have become popular with genres similar to related titles, such as "The First Son of a Soup House."

Successful people always have a mentor.There is also a win-win strategy with people who have already succeeded with their hypothesis, such as a partner to compensate for their shortcomings, a mentor (mentor), or a supporter who encourages them. And keep repeating hypothesis-test-execution. While repeating, we consider the needs of consumers to be the most important.

Highlight 2 things that are different from each self-help book

'The 10,000-hour rule is wrong' vs. 'The 10,000-hour rule is right.'

'The 10,000-hour rule is wrong.'

First. It depends. If you were an athlete, yes. However, there is no correlation between years of experience and skill. The quickest way to gain expertise is to find a good mentor and learn the rules of effective success. It's not about how much time, it's about how you spend it. The relationship between expertise and time means that quality is more important than quantity. It is said that the time of experience is not closely related to success. (It's more important how you learn in training with a teacher.)

'You have to do the 10,000-hour rule'

He said that there is nothing to enjoy, and that when there is sweat and hardship due to crazy efforts, it will pay off with luck.

'Dig only one well' vs 'Dig a variety of wells'

'A Well'

Sometimes we try too many things and end up not developing a solid skill in one area. As a result, it's hard to learn new skills even if you want to. We have started a business motivated by freedom, but freedom becomes our burden.

'Various wells'

It is said that successful people are hybrids. The author says that it is more appropriate to dig several wells than just one. It is said that Korean masters do not define themselves by this field, that field, or profession, but have superior knowledge in all fields.

The most difficult area: execution

When you read their books, your brain and mind change temporarily, and you feel a sense of purpose and motivation. However, passion and will are difficult to continue to practice with passion and will alone because the brain has not adapted to the fast times in the process of human evolution, and the primitive brain still remains. That's why all self-help books emphasize the area of practice at the end. Even if a company has a lot of ideas and goals, such as "I want to do YouTube," "I want to start a business," "I want to be a streamer," "I want to make a pipeline," and so on, very few people put them into practice. And this is natural to human instincts and brains, so you don't have to blame yourself. It's a way to raise your practice.

Steps to Quit

1. Have a high sense of purpose. Ask yourself specifically about your philosophical doubts. Let's make complexity simple.

2. Break down your high sense of purpose into sub-goals. There is a well-known way to be-become. It becomes a strong sense of purpose. In order to become, it is to create a ladder that leads to "what you need to do now," "what you need to do tomorrow," and "the end goal."

3. It's a way to create a routine. If your goal was to exercise today and you didn't create a routine,

4. It's a way to design your environment. Even if you are running with a high sense of purpose, designing routines and environments, wandering will come again. If you give your brain a good rest before you run again, it will remember your previous routine with more potential and originality, and it will give you a sweeter product than before. Practice is a difficult area for everyone, so let's work step by step to improve our ability to execute.

check point
(Specific Questions)

If your goal is to quit, or if you want to have a strong sense of purpose through the becoming-do method, write down sub-goals that you can implement right away. Then you have a ladder from a sub-goal that you can run to right now.

On the Decline of Civil Service Popularity and the MZ Generation's Exodus...

Navigating the Journey: From Civil Servant to Aspiring Entrepreneur...

The motivation and end destination are different when someone has to run for money, for success, for a family, for love and so on. Just as each person runs at a different pace and in different directions, the disposition and culture of the two organizations, the large corporations and the civil servants, were different. And now, while trying to start a business, he lives with a different mindset than an office worker. However, at least those in their 20s~30s think that it is too old to just live without getting to know themselves.

No matter what kind of job it is, it's a personal choice: "Find a job that matches your inclinations by getting to know yourself, or find a job with a sense of purpose." However, I believe that in order to be happy, you have to go through the process of getting to know yourself. This is because we are all faced with problems by the waves of life, and the choices we make next can be seen as a product of our own experiences. It's not bad to be willing to compromise with the world, but I wish there were more people who lived their lives in their own colors and not in the eyes of others...I wrote about the organization of examinees and civil servants.

I felt sorry for the incumbents who were working diligently, but I wanted the examinees to find a 'job' that suited their inclinations rather than preparing for the short-term and civil service exams just for the purpose of finding a job without thinking about it. I've also failed to start a business one after another, and I've become a person who is looking for 'work' instead of 'job', so the responsibility that comes with autonomy is very great. However, I decided to use the past of failure as an experience to see a positive future. From the perspective of others, I have been in a large company and a civil servant related to my major. No big deal...Don't think that employment is the only way to solve your problems, and I would like to see a country where young people take on various challenges according to the end goal, but I don't think it will be possible at that time. I'm young, too, but people don't care about others.

Regarding the decline in the popularity of civil servants and the rush to leave MZ...

There are no people who are thinking about leaving the company because of the popularity of civil servants and the view of society, right? The civil service profession is a profession whose preferences change depending on the game. Since the IMF, the popularity of civil servants has been rising, peaking, and on a sharp downward spiral. It's hard to do it these days, right?

Even during my tenure, some of the incumbents whose popularity has been on a downward spiral, and some of them look depressed when they look at the people who have left the company, saying, "Is this the right job for me?" However, the popularity of civil servants goes up with the economic cycle. It is true that the corona economy and the presidential election overlapped and a lot of money was released, and the wage gap between public companies and large corporations widened due to inflation in line with the inflation rate. Due to the increase in interest rates in the United States, our country also quickly withdrew funds from the market. Of course, at the May FOMC meeting, the US will most likely moderate QT (quantitative tightening) at the May FOMC meeting, as growth is supported. However, Korea does not have a very high growth rate, and is quite sensitive to 3,000 trillion trillion in household debt (including pre-tax and loans to financial institutions) and deflation (economic recession), which can be a time bomb.

The Bank of Korea has moderated the pace of interest rate hikes, but the difference between short- and long-term interest rates has reversed like in the U.S., usually according to the business cycle.

The moment a recession sets in, the preference of civil servants rises again. This is the only job that provides legal protection. I hope you don't have the foolish thing of thinking about leaving the company just because your popularity is declining. I don't think anyone changes jobs based on salary alone, but if you apply it as a factor in turnover and quitting, I think it can be a short-term perspective.

That's just defining one's profession in the eyes of society. Decision to leave the company and move forward after leaving the company The area of practice is difficult for everyone, and it is natural to have three days of determination, so you need to design your own environment and practice the area of practice. Still, if you're thinking about quitting with a high sense of purpose...I hope you live selfishly for yourself at least once.

I appreciate it.